— THE —
CHIRON EFFECT

"Lisa Tahir brings astrological wisdom to life through reliable psychology. She speaks with honesty and passion, revealing traces of her own battle scars. Relatable, beautiful, and profound."

BENJAMIN W. DECKER, AUTHOR OF
PRACTICAL MEDITATION FOR BEGINNERS

"In her groundbreaking book, *The Chiron Effect*, Lisa Tahir skillfully accompanies readers on a powerful journey to heal our deepest wounds. By sharing her personal story—as well as effective methods to break old trauma-based patterns, harness our minds for positive change, and embody unconditional love—Lisa teaches us how to become the free and joyful people we were always meant to be."

MYRA GOODMAN, COAUTHOR OF *QUEST FOR ETERNAL SUNSHINE:
A HOLOCAUST SURVIVOR'S JOURNEY FROM DARKNESS TO LIGHT*

"As an astrologer I have always found Chiron to be both a key to understanding the wounds we repeat and the guide to living out our soul's purpose. There has never been, until now, a book that guides astrologers, healing practitioners, and readers alike to articulating that purpose. In *The Chiron Effect*, Tahir offers a brilliant synthesis of psychology and astrology, but most of all she offers hope for the healing of our souls."

MARI SELBY, AUTHOR OF *LIGHTNING STRIKES TWICE*

"Lisa Tahir writes beautifully about the journey inward, where one can find their greatest power by having the courage and self-compassion to heal their core wounds."

ORA NADRICH, FOUNDER/PRESIDENT OF THE INSTITUTE FOR TRANSFORMATIONAL THINKING AND AUTHOR OF *SAYS WHO?* AND *LIVE TRUE*

"This book is a tender, kind, and compassionate journey into how we heal our core wounds. It blends and weaves astrology with self-help healing, creating an integrated approach to the healing of the self. It is useful and timely."

RONALD A. ALEXANDER, PH.D., AUTHOR OF *WISE MIND, OPEN MIND* AND EXECUTIVE DIRECTOR OF OPENMIND TRAINING INSTITUTE, SANTA MONICA, CA

"Lisa Tahir integrates her deep understanding of personal transformation with a compassionate, insightful, and practical view of the meaning of astrological Chiron. This is a much-needed and powerful resource of healing tools for practitioners and laypeople alike."

PATRICIA MAHER, HMC, MSW, ASTROLOGER AND HOMEOPATH

"With *The Chiron Effect,* Lisa Tahir presents a clear guide and gentle invitation to reveal and decode old, unhealthy patterns and apply the salve of empathy and forgiveness. Lisa remains approachable to the reader with her vulnerable and straightforward writing style. She illuminates a clear depth-process through which we may each awaken our beautiful inner healer and heal core wounding—a deep and accessible resource."

COREY FOLSOM, RELATIONSHIP COACH, LOS ANGELES, CA

THE

CHIRON EFFECT

Healing Our Core Wounds through Astrology, Empathy, and Self-Forgiveness

Lisa Tahir, LCSW

Bear & Company
Rochester, Vermont

Bear & Company
One Park Street
Rochester, Vermont 05767
www.BearandCompanyBooks.com

Text stock is SFI certified

Bear & Company is a division of Inner Traditions International

Note to the reader: *This book is intended as an informational guide. The remedies, approaches, and techniques described herein are meant to supplement, and not to be a substitute for, professional medical care or treatment. They should not be used to treat a serious ailment without prior consultation with a qualified health care professional.*

Cataloging-in-Publication Data for this title is available from the Library of Congress

ISBN 978-1-59143-395-8 (print)
ISBN 978-1-59143-396-5 (ebook)

Printed and bound in the United States by Lake Book Manufacturing, Inc. The text stock is SFI certified. The Sustainable Forestry Initiative® program promotes sustainable forest management.

10 9 8 7 6 5 4 3 2

Text design and layout by Virginia Scott Bowman
This book was typeset in Garamond Premier Pro, Legacy Sans, and Gill Sans with Kapra Neue Pro and Avant Garde Gothic used as display typefaces

To send correspondence to the author of this book, mail a first-class letter to the author c/o Inner Traditions • Bear & Company, One Park Street, Rochester, VT 05767, and we will forward the communication, or contact the author directly at **www.nolatherapy.com.**

This book is dedicated to those of you who are learning the value of being happy over being right; who view your missteps and challenges as opportunities to become a more evolved and happier version of yourself; to you who are consciousness shifters; and to you who have journeyed to the inner depths of life, love, and loss, yet have chosen to rise from the dark nights of your soul with a beautifully scarred yet open heart—a heart filled with the desire to forgive yourself and others, so that you may love and be loved more deeply.

❧❧

I am grateful to each of you who have come to me disguised as my client, family member, friend, lover, or stranger in the street, only to remind me of the reality that we are all connected, united by our humanity. You have shined a light upon my path, which has illuminated my heart with greater humility, peace, happiness, and the wisdom to choose only love.

My intention is to be a vessel for Spirit's messages and a light of guidance in this world so that I may add to the eternally growing narrative and conversation about emotional healing and spiritual development. May we each linger longer and listen to our inner voice, encouraging us to deeper awareness. Whatever you have been through, don't silence yourself. Take risks to be authentic, for there you will find your courage.

⋇⧼⧽⋇

The planet does not need more successful people. The planet desperately needs more peacemakers, healers, restorers, storytellers, and lovers of all kinds.
His Holiness the 14th Dalai Lama

⋇⧼⧽⋇

And so it is, and so it shall be,
in all directions,
and in every dimension.
Amen.

Contents

Acknowledgments

Mom and Dad, you have taught me my most valuable life lessons about forgiveness and happiness; thank you for co-creating my foundation in unconditional love.

I am the oldest of five unique siblings, all of whom I love deeply. I appreciate you, Ashley (my dear Seester), for being the rock I can depend upon. Ruby, you are actually a step-in mother who has enlivened my family with your humor and spirit. We are a dynamically blended Pakistani-American family, and my favorite memories are with all of you in my New Orleans home laughing hysterically about anything!

I am also blessed by the presence of a second family and mentorship found in Gene and Mary Koss. Thank you, Gene, for gifting me with glass art as a way of healing through creating, and by believing in me.

Since I was a child I have wanted to work in the field of psychology. I've gone through many iterations of myself since my parents found a note I had scribbled when I was five. It read: "I want to be a psychiatrist." As it turns out, the challenges and gifts of being a healer have been the driving force in creating my life.

There is a sacred intimacy to the therapeutic relationship. With each step I take toward answering my call to be of service, I've grown into a woman of deeper integrity. Thank you to each and every client for choosing me to walk with you through the deep valleys of your soul. My heart has been with you each step and will be forevermore.

I have cultivated a circle of spiritual mothers who have supported me as both mentors and sisters. They are Ora Nadrich, Katherine Woodward Thomas, Marianne Williamson, Prem Glidden, and Debra Voelker. As strong, authentic women, your power comes from the spiritual truths you each embody and live by. As a result I have been blessed by the generosity of your wisdom. Thank you.

❖❖❖

I have found a spiritual home as a member of the Self-Realization Fellowship in Pacific Palisades, California, which was founded by Paramahansa Yogananda in 1950. I have spent the last few years taking walks on its beautiful grounds that surround Lake Shrine and meditating in its Windmill Chapel. Miraculous changes have transpired in my life as a result. "Dedicated to the upliftment of humanity through prayer" is a tenet taught by Yogananda that I believe in and live by. I have directed healing energy to others, including those of you reading this book. I am grateful to be a part of this spiritual community and want to acknowledge the power and alignment I have found through my devotion.

Thank you, Gary Reggio and Robert Nehlig, my web designers and trusted collaborators. I appreciate your innovation, focused creativity, and support for my work over the years.

Peter Hough, thank you for your knowledge and expertise in helping me with this book. You and your wife, Claire Candy Hough, are wonderful friends and inspirational creators who enrich my life.

Mari Selby, your wisdom as my editor, contributor, and collaborator to this book has been invaluable.

Jennet Inglis, thank you for your prodigious and meticulous attention to detail in the editing of my book, and the clarity you brought to it. Thank you, Margie Baxley, for adding touches and details to this manuscript.

Gratitude to you, Robert Weinberg, Esq., for your legal guidance and intellectual banter.

I'd like to thank you, Matteo Neivert, for being an inspiration to me through this writing process through our artistic collaborations throughout the years.

My publisher, Inner Traditions, has brought this work out into the world. I am grateful for your co-creation with me in reaching people with Chiron's message of forgiveness and self-healing. I thank you, Jon Graham, for discovering and selecting my book for publication, and Kelly Bowen, for a positive contract negotiation experience. Meghan MacLean, you have made editing fun, dare I say, through your supportive style and guidance. Thank you, Manzanita Carpenter Sanz, for scheduling upcoming and ongoing events that connect readers with this information. The support you have each given me in bringing this work to the mainstream for people everywhere to access is cherished.

And Randy Peyser, your commitment, expertise, and direction as my agent has brought this book into the hands of so many, and I am grateful for you and your efforts.

INTRODUCTION

Chiron and Psychoastrology®

A school shooting; a drunk driver taking an innocent life; the loss of a job, a loved one, or a relationship . . . now more than ever people turn to therapists, spiritual healers, and countless other professionals for support and healing. Yet those of us who work to relieve the emotional pain of humanity have shortcomings of our own—even as we serve our highest calling.

Chiron was discovered in 1977 by American astronomer Charles T. Kowal from images taken at Palomar Observatory in San Diego, California. Chiron has the unusual characteristic of features like both an asteroid and a comet. It was recognized as the first object in the centaur class. Centaurs are objects with unstable orbits, and Chiron remains one of the largest such worlds known. It was initially classified as an asteroid and as a minor planet, 2060 Chiron. Today it is classified as both a minor planet and a comet and is known by the cometary designation 95P/Chiron. This book that you are now holding accurately identifies twelve areas of core wounding, diagnosed by the astrological placement of Chiron in the reader's birth chart. It is this placement of Chiron that identifies the causes for people to repeat painful, unconscious patterns.

In our astrological natal chart, also our called birth chart, the location of Chiron reveals these core wounds, which block our capacity to have self-empathy and to forgive. Lack of empathy and compassion for ourselves and others obstructs our ability to both create and allow our desires. By working with Chiron, I was able to come to understand the correlation between my deepest inner wounding and my greatest challenges. I trademarked the modality Psychoastrology® to demarcate the interrelationship between our personal psychology and our natal astrology. The insights and healing I have found for myself inspired me to share them with you, the reader, so that you, too, will be equipped to identify and heal your core wounds through an empowerment process. Thus you can then remove obstacles and blocks and, in doing so, create the life you really want to live through your conscious choices.

Why Chiron?

In Greek mythology, Chiron the centaur is acknowledged as being the founding father and discoverer of the healing arts, botany, pharmacy, the science of herbs, and medicine. Chiron tutored Achilles and Asclepius in the medical and healing arts. He enjoyed a good life on Mt. Pelion until one fateful day.

As the story goes, an arrow poisoned by the blood of the Hydra mistakenly struck Chiron in his leg, causing him excruciating pain. The agony he experienced put him in touch with the fragility of humanity. Finding it unbearable to live with the pain he experienced continually and unable to heal himself, Chiron asked Zeus if he could trade his immortality with Prometheus and give up his life. Zeus granted his wish.

Chiron took his place among the gods, where he became the archetype of the wounded healer.

Being a centaur, Chiron embodies both human consciousness and animal instinct. When we are wounded our innate animalistic instinct for self-protection kicks in as a means of survival. Initially this is a natural and necessary coping strategy. But many of us dwell too long in this space, therefore separating ourselves from our source of inner wisdom and intuition.

The mythological story of Chiron represents the psychoastrological invitation to journey inward and bring greater understanding, healing, and power to your life. Almost everyone has an aspect of life wherein they seem to repeat the same frustrating patterns and, at the same time, continuously wonder how to change.

In early psychoanalytic literature Freud was the first to name these recurring and painful, cyclical patterns. The *repetition compulsion* has been written about in various ways since Freud coined the term in 1914. Erik Erikson, the renowned psychoanalyst who fathered the stages of psychosocial development, wrote about *destiny neurosis* in *Childhood and Society,* "the way that some people make the same mistakes over and over . . . the individual unconsciously arranges for variations of an original theme which he has not learned either to overcome or to live with." Object relations theory teaches that object relations (the relationships we had with our primary caretakers) early in life may be unconsciously repeated. In his book *Further Learning from the Patient,* British psychoanalyst Patrick Casement notes, "Unresolved conflicts continue to generate attempts at solutions which do not really work . . . until a genuine solution is found." And attachment theorists believe that early development patterns form schemas of relationship that are repeated. A schema is the mental representation of relationships, which becomes organized and encoded as experiential and cognitive data.

In the astrological chart, Chiron is found in one of the twelve signs of the zodiac: Aries, Taurus, Gemini, Cancer, Leo, Virgo, Libra, Scorpio, Sagittarius, Capricorn, Aquarius, or Pisces. The placement of Chiron in a zodiac sign reveals the specific core wound that causes recurring issues, themes, and problems that result in persistent, painful challenges and patterns as a result.

Additionally, the astrological *house* that Chiron is found in represents one of twelve distinct sectors/areas of one's life wherein one's core wound manifests. Here is an overview: The first house relates to our physical body and our personality; the second house has to do with our finances and moral value system; the third house deals with communication, siblings, and childhood; the fourth house pertains to how we were nurtured and conditioned, our home (both family of origin home and our current home); the fifth house relates to creativity, romance, legacy, and play; the sixth house has to do with work, health, and our routines (structure); the seventh house addresses contracts—both intimate (marriage and relationships) and professional; the eighth house has to do with power, sex, and other people's money; the ninth house involves religion, philosophy, foreign travel, and education; the tenth house has to do with career, reputation, and image; the eleventh house is all about friends, groups, associates, and community; and last, the twelfth house has to do with the unconscious mind, shadow self (addictions, jails, hospitals), and spirituality.

Like a raw nerve, the house placement of Chiron describes what parts of our lives we might edit or hide for fear of being rejected or not accepted by others. Chiron's house placement also reveals the areas of sensitivity where we are triggered. Like a soothing balm, Chiron's placement in one of the twelve houses has the potential—and the power—to heal our negative reactivity to both the outside world and within ourselves.

Using the twelve signs of the zodiac and the twelve houses of our natal chart, we can locate Chiron's core wounding in our lives and identify specific personal challenges as they pertain to our particular wounds. Through this understanding of psychoastrology you will discover how the root causes of your wounding can become the source of your greatest healing and empowerment.

The purpose of this book is twofold. The first purpose is, again, to reveal the unconscious patterns sourced in your core wounding. The second purpose is to learn how to heal those places through empathy and self-forgiveness. In this psychoastrological process there is hope that you will resolve much of your suffering, end self-sabotage, and finally be free to create and allow your life to unfold in new ways. You can use this information for yourself, your partner, or a loved one or in your practice as a healing professional.

By having the courage and taking the time to progressively attend to the wounded parts of myself, I continue to undergo profound transformation. By working with Chiron we find the ability to cultivate great psychological, emotional, and spiritual strength formerly inaccessible to us. *The Chiron Effect* reveals how to transcend the shadowed restrictive limitations that cause unhappiness and deplete our power.

It seems significant that the legend of Chiron tells of a poisonous arrow mistakenly striking our hero of the healing arts. Of course, in modern times one would not be literally struck with an arrow shot from a bow. However, being struck by an arrow is a metaphor for the unexpected—when something seems to come out of nowhere!

Chiron asked Zeus if he could die because the pain of his unexpected trauma was too much to bear. How often have you in your own heart and mind wished for an ending of pain created by circumstances beyond your ability to cope? Some of you reading this now may have wanted to take your life in order to stop the pain created by others or yourself. The gift of Chiron's psychoastrology is that it's within our ability to heal through empathy and self-forgiveness. As we heal, comfort is found through the inner voice that offers us understanding, encouragement, and compassion.

The Chiron Effect

The *Chiron effect* is a term I developed to describe the magnetic pull or *orbit* we have in and around specific areas of core wounding and vulnerability. The problems we have typically cluster around core issues and themes. An *orbit* is a pattern that we have grown accustomed to living within, thus becoming a set frequency. *Effect* is defined as a change that is a result or consequence of an action or other cause. Therefore, when we change our orbit, we affect our frequency. We are beings of habituation; ourselves orbiting our surroundings, as well as being orbit-surrounded by people, places, and things. Our routine, habits, people, places, and things make up the orbit that we inhabit through our actions and choices. Notice the people in your life, the experiences that you find yourself in consistently; this is the orbit that gravitates toward and surrounds you. We are each planets in the solar system of our own lives.

The Chiron effect offers you a way of decoding the underlying factors influencing the magnetic pull (orbit) that keeps you in the same pattern and frequency of your identified problems. Second, you are invited into a depth-process of healing to shift your current frequency.

Let's take a look at ourselves through the lens of Chiron. Everyone has wounds. Everyone has experienced loss, disappointment, sadness, depression, rejection, or a taking away of or a letting go of what was once meaningful to us. We are each acquainted with suffering. We have all felt pain—whether it's physical, emotional, mental, spiritual—or any combination thereof.

It is our *human* condition to experience wounding on the earthly plane of existence. It is our *celestial* condition to embody healing during our earthly tenure of existence. To extrapolate from the famous philosopher and Jesuit priest Pierre Teilhard de Chardin, because we are spiritual beings having a human experience, the dissemination of healing is administered in each of three dimensions composing the self: body, soul, and spirit.

When undertaking to heal in this way, initially it is very important to ensure that we have reliable and varied coping mechanisms, self-care strategies, and natural supports in place before and during our exploration of core wounding. We need to expose and explore these deep wounds carefully and gently while developing adequate natural supports and concrete practices of self-nurturing. Thus, a toolbox of coping strategies and an array of self-soothing behaviors and practices are some of the first things to develop and implement. Creating a quiet and peaceful emotional environment to do this healing work is your first step. Identify a comfortable location, utilize a notebook or journal, and perhaps ensure that you have a special candle to light as you work through the stages of healing that this book will walk you through.

Healing your core wounds begins with allowing a space for forgiveness within yourself and is reinforced by creating a supportive external environment for your journey.

In addition to identifying and healing your specific psychoastrology of core wounding—illuminated by the sign and house placement of Chiron in your natal chart—Chiron will bring other dynamics to the forefront of your awareness. These include the shadow-aspect dynamics of self-defeating practices, patterns, and behaviors, which will be highlighted so that you may see how they have been operating in the background of your life.

How to Approach This Book

Every chapter in this book is written to build on the next. It is not unlike cooking a complex dish whereby layers of flavors are built on each other—such as salt, smoke, spice, sugar, citrus, or umami. In order to create a balanced end result, and if you wish to glean the most life-changing and long-lasting benefits, it is important to read from the first page onward without skipping any passages.

I have found that I relate to every sign placement of Chiron in some fashion. My main issues come from the placement of Chiron in a specific sign and house; however, we heal ancillary wounds by studying *all* of the sign and house placements of Chiron. This thorough knowledge of psychoastrology makes us more adaptable, resilient, and prepared. Each chapter offers insights, approaches, and techniques for healing that I have researched and utilized over the past two decades as a licensed clinical social worker. I want you to master self-healing so that you can live happily in the present moment, thereby being open to all that is available to you.

Personal growth and development are a lot like baking; both are an art and a science. You can't rush a cake to bake no matter how long you may stand over it, watching it or turning up the temperature to rush it along. Either the person watching it will become frustrated or the bottom of the cake will burn and leave the center cold. Similarly, invest the requisite time to learn about your core wounds presented within these pages.

As stated in William Shakespeare's play *Julius Caesar,* "The fault, dear Brutus, is not in our stars, but in ourselves, that we are underlings." I use astrology as the diagnostic tool to identify core wounding, but the prescription and remediation involve a combination of psychology, spirituality, *and* personal responsibility. This is the inner journey into your own psychoastrology. Awareness is the first step in awakening to Chiron, the beautiful inner healer. I wrote this book because I want to encourage you to express your dreams. I want to inspire you to speak your voice, live into your life; this one life that you have to create on *this* time/space continuum. Honor your existence by completing what you came here for. Don't cave inward for longer than the time it takes to regroup and rise to greet your challenges with the resilience that is embedded within your heart. Don't compromise your voice, vision, or values. Do be open to new ideas and suggestions.

Refute the information of those who tell you your dream isn't possible, it's too costly or impractical, or they . . . simply can't help you. Lean inward to find the reservoir of unlimited potential that you possess. Close your eyes, and play the music in *your* heart. Deeply root yourself into your value and worth because you are good enough right *now*. Even when you don't feel good enough or haven't done your best, you are a spiritually perfect being and you are lovable.

I personally and professionally became frustrated with lengthy assessment and treatment processes that involved years of rehashing troubling and traumatic memories. Rehashing the past only produced gnawing feelings of disempowerment. With a desire to address my own core wounding, I sought alternative assessment methods and turned to meditation.

During meditation I received a message: Research Chiron and expand upon the wounded healer mythology. I was invited to familiarize myself with all aspects related to this archetype, especially the notion of individual core wounding. Finally, I was encouraged to add to the narrative of healing by sharing my research and personal journey in this book. I found that in developing *The Chiron Effect*, what is offered here works in concert with the alternative and prevailing methodologies known to date.

I am conscious and respectful of the diversity within our humanity, and I want to acknowledge those differences among us now. My work is applicable to and inclusive of one's race, ethnicity, gender identification, age, national orientation, sexual orientation, disability, socioeconomic background, status, religious belief, and spiritual practice. I want to bring us together through a dialogue of healing. I am a student of *A Course in Miracles,* a book scribed by Helen Schucman and published in 1976 by the Foundation for Inner Peace. It is a curriculum for those seeking spiritual transformation by shifting from a thought system based on fear to a thought system based on love. Meditation and prayer are a part of my daily self-care, and I enjoy studying the metaphysical, spiritual, psychological, and quantum fields. I call upon God/Universal Intelligence/Source Energy/Jesus/Spirit to be with me and assist me in all aspects of my personal and professional lives. I appreciate that everyone has different belief systems.

I want to acknowledge your diversity in thought and the belief systems that accompany you as my reader, and I invite you to apply your *own* belief system to this work. There are many names, ways, and paths that may be utilized to arrive at a common destination. I encourage you to tailor the language in this book to assist and serve you.

Finding Safety in an Unsafe World

When our familiar way of living (i.e., people, places, or things) falls apart there is a breakdown in trusting that we are safe and grounded. There is a fractured sense of stability in realizing that our predictable world is no more. This phenomenon is most often experienced as emotional distress, much like when grieving a loss or a death.

As the initial shock and disbelief of what's happened begins to wear off, there is a sense of disorientation from opposing feelings of numbness alternating with a flood of emotions. Our prior operating system becomes obsolete, and we are left standing in unknown territory.

As humans we have been conditioned to react to and fear what is challenging or unfamiliar. Commonly known as "fight, flight, or freeze," these automatic responses do not align with feelings of stability, security, and safety—all of which are needed to function optimally.

It takes courage to go within and face fear, panic, and unexpected shifts that suddenly change the landscape and the predictable knowledge of our world. However, when we move closer to our inner wounding, we come nearer to our deepest needs and desires, which have often been stuck in a holding pattern yearning to be noticed, seen, and heard. I encourage you to give yourself permission to *feel into* this information that is available and contained within your core wounding.

Initially, moving closer to our inner wounding feels counterintuitive, but it holds the key to our complete healing. Through this process we begin to repattern ourselves. We gain clarity and develop inner strength.

For example, when we touch a hand to a hot stove, the natural and instinctive biological response is to pull our hand away immediately and never revisit that experience again. It is an appropriate biological defense to keep us from being burned repeatedly.

Emotionally speaking, people may stay in an unfulfilling relationship (a metaphor for a hand on the hot stove) for so long that their emotions (nerve endings) become numb or even deadened. What started as a pang of warning becomes full-blown hurt that can numb you emotionally over time, given that you may have minimized or even ignored your intuition. Instead of choosing to face the many fears that naturally and inherently accompany change, this pain-point experience can become the norm for you as the gradual slide into self-deception begins in order to maintain the relationship rather than using your energy to start over or be single again.

Our wounds are the way in which the Divine makes contact with us in order to wake us up to an aspect of self that needs to be excavated and healed. We experience this communication through our body. The body is a symptom bearer of how we are living. Chronic physical and emotional problems are communicating imbalances or *wounds* to get our attention.

These sensitive places need to be addressed and explored with compassion. Our wounding activates a deeper transpersonal process within that is discoverable through an understanding of the psychoastrology of Chiron. Often it is through pain that we focus our attention on what's really needed. With curiosity and concern, this deeper look within is the path that actually leads us to our happiness.

Awakening

Chiron is both the gateway for, and invitation to, the development of empathy. Carl Jung describes the wounded healer as embodying both the spirit of compassion and of selflessness. In its most positive aspect, the wounded healer symbolizes the potentially transformative power within that is ready and willing to heal our core wounds.

Unaddressed, the wounds of Chiron play like a hidden narrative running in the backdrop of our lives, creating problems that we don't understand. Psychiatrist Carl Jung wrote in *Memories, Dreams, Reflections,* "until you make the unconscious conscious, it will direct your life and you will call it fate." Chiron encourages us to take personal responsibility for our own fate. In recognizing our shared bond of human vulnerability, we become a wellspring of compassion and support for ourselves and also for those whose lives we touch.

1

Living Deeply into Each Moment

When I was a little girl, I would lie in bed and read the Bible with my grandmother, Mildred Colbert Webb, or Mimi, as I called her. I was fascinated by the verses in Proverbs. One night I remember asking, "Mimi, what does it mean that 'He who curses his father or his mother, His lamp will go out in time of darkness?' Mimi, why do 'those who guard their mouths and their tongues keep themselves from trouble?'"

Mimi's spectacles would scoot down low, almost falling off her nose as she replied. "Well, Lisa, you're too young to be concerned with these things, but adults hurt each other with their words, and you can't take those things back once they are said. The Bible is teaching you to be careful with the words you speak; that's all, sugar. You don't have to worry about that now, dear. I love you so much; let's go to bed."

I whispered, "I love you, too, Mimi." With the scent of Sucrets menthol on her breath, I curled into her embrace. Enveloped in safety, we both feel asleep.

What memories might be peeking out of your consciousness at this moment as you read my words? Allow yourself to be nostalgic. Take a moment to reflect back and write down in your journal memory impressions that you have of your childhood, both positive and negative. What do you notice about them? Which memories evoke more emotion from you now? Put a star next to those. Use this list as an evolving template of memories as you continue reading. You can use the positive memories to evoke feelings of love, joy, and delight when you want to conjure those emotions. Take the painful memories and work with them using the self-soothing practices and techniques offered as you continue to learn more about your core wounding identified by Chiron. This evolving list will be beneficial for you to release the residual pain and shift the beliefs you made about yourself because of them.

As a young girl, I didn't know that my interest in and hunger for spiritual truth was born while reading Proverbs with Mimi. In hindsight, that was the beginning of my interest in personal development. My grandparents were the pillars of my life. I was graced with them as my touchstones of unconditional love. When do you recall becoming interested in psychospiritual, self-help, astrological, philosophical, quantum, or metaphysical topics? Why was that hunger birthed within you, what answers have you wanted to find, and have you found them? Take some time to journal what comes up for you. The answers to these questions relate to the ways that you find and develop meaning and purpose for your life.

In later years, my childhood and adolescence would be marked by emotional, physical, and sexual abuse and related hardships, which I took out on myself (as many adult survivors of trauma do) in subsequent years through self-harm that was a result of my low self-esteem. However, I am learning to love myself unconditionally through the practices and methods found in the pages of this book. I invite you to find self-compassion and healing for yourself here too.

What early experiences caused you to feel unconditionally loved? Who were the people involved with those feelings, and are you still in touch with them now? Do you carry deeply imprinted memory impressions of being hurt, rejected, abandoned, or abused? I suggest that you envelop and surround yourself with compassion and love for the little one that you once were. At the same time, hold a space of nonjudgmental acceptance for yourself and all that you have lived through. As you engage in your psychoastrological healing you will learn to create new stories from your past that support, nurture, and encourage you.

For many of us who are drawn to the healing professions, oftentimes we are motivated in part by our desire to heal ourselves. That is why we practitioners, almost always, truly are . . . wounded healers.

Memory Impressions

As a way to heal my core wounding through creativity, I use glass as an artistic medium to express myself nonverbally. Casting glass is a process whereby hot molten glass is removed from a 2300°F furnace and poured into sand, steel, or wood molds made by the artist beforehand. I enjoy the physical process of creating these pieces, as it takes me to another place mentally that has always felt good. Through my glass artwork, I have found part of my own therapy and self-care. As an artist, I have sought to capture the emotion and representation of unconditional love through a glass casting I've created entitled, "Memory Impressions." These pieces are representations of my belief that it is unconditional love that connects us all to each other. I visually imagine crystallizing unconditional love into mass and form through these creations. To represent in physical form the sheer number of memories that we share during our lifespan, I have made thousands of "Memory Impression" pieces. As they hang on the wall or rest on a tabletop in the owner's space, a part of my energy and heart lives within each piece. I like to imagine that my energy infuses the space with blessings and unconditional love.

The act of creating is a genesis. Genesis is a beginning, the process of becoming. Who are you becoming? What creative processes can you use to heal and express your authentic self? Reflect upon them now and write them down. Do you dedicate time each week for your craft? Is there a secret passion you want to express? What have you wanted to try but haven't? Would you like to create those possibilities for yourself now? If you would, take time after reading today to begin that process. Not all of us express ourselves through the spoken word. Some of you may dance, sing, paint, write—there are infinite possibilities for leaning into this part of yourself and giving it your full attention.

Reiki Healing and Giving Back

Since becoming a Reiki Level II practitioner in 2015, I have imparted Reiki healing energy into the art I create. My work carries an intention for healing. I ask you to discover similar ways to express yourself creatively and set the intention now to make time for it, for it's important that we share our gifts and abilities with others.

This may manifest by giving back to your community through a public charity, as a volunteer, or the way you make yourself available to a neighbor, friend, or stranger. You may decide to start a volunteer tradition in your city once a year, or hand out bottles of water during summer months to the countless homeless people who populate the street corners of our cities and towns.

Perhaps you sit on the board of a nonprofit or have started one yourself. There are as many ways to give back and be of service as there are people in the world. Find what resonates with you and do that, be that, speak that. As Gandhi said, "You must be the change you want to see in the world."

I've learned through much trial and error that *we* can be the embodiment of unconditional love for ourselves, and that we have the choice to demonstrate that love through our choices, every single day. The choices we make source their origin within our personal value system. What values are most important to you? Without judgment take time to write them down. Another way to ask yourself this is, "What are my priorities? How do I want to be known? How will I be remembered? How do I *want* to be remembered?"

I've asked myself to enhance my personal integrity by aligning my actions in congruence with my beliefs. I am going to ask you, right now, to consider making a commitment to yourself in your own way. You may want to reevaluate the degree to which you are showing up for yourself and for others. You may choose to take risks to be more authentic in your personal or professional lives. Psychoastrology will help you to understand the relationship between your core wounding and the degree to which you are living in congruence with what is truly important to you, thus giving you the power to make changes as you see fit.

Finding Your Voice

When I started the process of writing this book my greatest challenge surprised me. It wasn't my lack of knowledge, nor was it my lack of research. My greatest challenge was not whether I was making a fresh contribution to the greater narrative of healing by bringing the archetype of Chiron to life. No, none of these issues were problematic.

What was difficult was to find and articulate my *own* voice. I was afraid to share my self. Our core wounding can trigger feelings of shame. By healing through empathy and self-forgiveness, I found the courage to share some of my experiences with you, my reader, so that we may connect in that shared space of authenticity and human vulnerability.

How do you respond when you are unexpectedly face-to-face with criticisms and judgments that are either imposed on you by others or imposed on you by your own limited thinking? I had to answer this question in order to personally embody the twelve core wounds of Chiron so that I could then write about them. I finally realized that the writing of this book was a gift of healing in disguise, and when I had this insight, a feeling of deep peace came over me. My inner self spoke to me and said, "Lisa Tahir, you know you can do this. Be patient, and let this book come forth through you."

At this I said out loud, "Yes, but where is *my* voice in this work?"

My inner voice encouragingly chimed in, "Your core wounding has been in the area of knowing your own 'value and worth,' and as you develop a stronger connection to the teacher that is within you, and trust yourself to share the wisdom that you know, the words will flow from your fingertips onto these pages. Your value lies within, and you are absolutely good enough: Trust yourself!"

I likewise encourage you to lean in to your inner knowing and communicate your truth, even though you may fear the level of vulnerability that this engenders in you. I focused on upgrading the messages of my self-talk, and I suggest that you begin to make your innermost dialogue a best friend. I said things to myself such as, "Well, you're writing this book to share a message of forgiveness and compassion, be courageous and speak your truth, share your experiences authentically, and then notice what happens." I have found that living authentically takes a commitment to living from a heart-centered place each day. That can be challenging, and some days are easier than others. It is helpful to speak lovingly to yourself and praise yourself for choosing your *own* authentic path—instead of judging yourself when you trip and stumble a bit by resorting to old habits. What possibilities do you imagine for yourself if you were to step *through* your fears of what others may think of you? If you were to express more and more of your authentic self? I encourage you to write these things down. What would you do? How does it feel to imagine being that version of yourself? Feel into those emotions now, and relish in the delight of imagining yourself having it, doing it, living it.

For me, the possibility I imagined for myself was to create a weekly podcast. I felt mind-blowing excitement and paralyzing fear in equal proportions at the same time just thinking about it! Now when I feel this concurrent set of emotions, I know it is a "yes" for me to move forward with that idea. I decided to face my fears head-on and, in March of 2016 I began a weekly podcast, *All Things Therapy,* on LA Talk Radio.

I've grown so much as a person because of this journey as an interviewer and a podcaster. I enjoy sharing messages of healing with you in this way through the show's mission statement to "Change Consciousness One Conversation at a Time." When we do something that scares us, that terrifies us, but that we also have a desire for, that is when we demonstrate courage.

Most all of us have practical wisdom to share, which has been gleaned from life experience, and I have found that we learn a lot from each other's stories. I have learned to trust in myself and my intuitive voice fully. This connection to our own inner being is one of our most valuable resources.

Through this work you will learn something about me, and a hell of a lot about yourself. I may be redundant at times; however, I know that we learn through repetition. We learn by hearing the same things expressed in different ways, over and over and over again. I hope that you become comfortable with unconditional self-love, acceptance, forgiveness, patience, compassion, and empathy, so that these qualities find a home deeply embedded inside of you.

In preparing and writing this book, I have held my own feet to the fire. What needed to be let go of was cleared as I allowed people, places, and things to fall away from my life. Let your inner wisdom guide you in deciding what needs to be burned away from within and without so that you may transform fully into the person you envision yourself being, at your very happiest. Allow the new and wonderful to fill your life.

I think that most of us have seen some of our hopes and dreams go up in smoke and tears only to rise from the ashes in new form, that of priceless treasures. The currency of transformative psychoastrology, spirituality, and rebirth is your entire heart, mind, and soul, and this is an all-in process. We are on a collective journey to delve into the mysteries of our core wounding and its healing. As we develop the strong inner musculature to support ourselves in this growth, Chiron meets us and shows us the way.

Hope

The ability to connect with and experience the feeling of hope is a fundamental predictor, which posits that we will succeed at accomplishing our desired goals. I want to inspire you to feel hopeful about your future because you can change any circumstance in your life with one small step at a time. I know, because I have changed the landscape of my own life and continue to do so with each passing day.

When I decided to open a second private practice in Los Angeles in 2014, I knew that I did not want to sell my home in New Orleans and move permanently to Los Angeles. I envisioned having two residences, one in New Orleans, Louisiana, and one in LA. I saw myself living between each city, enjoying the benefits of both.

At the time, however, I wasn't in a financial position to be able to afford the two residences I envisioned. I have learned we often hold a vision of our future with the accompanying desire, but not the obvious means to its accomplishment.

I advocate that we must step forward through our fear by initiating steps toward our vision to whatever degree we are able to effect at the time. Building upon our vision brick by brick, step by step, and drawing upon our remembrance of pulling through past hard times, we remain open to the hope that our current dream will come to fruition.

I decided to use what I learned when rebuilding from Hurricane Katrina and apply it to the life I wanted to create in Los Angeles. I'd been living in New Orleans when Hurricane Katrina hit the region in 2005. I used the emergency money I received from FEMA to rent a private office for psychotherapy in Baton Rouge, where I was evacuated to and living while New Orleans was underwater. While rebuilding my private practice remotely by doing phone sessions with clients who were also displaced, I lived in my office and showered at a nearby gym every day.

Likewise, initially I lived in my Los Angeles office on a pullout couch and showered each day at a 24 Hour Fitness gym. The owners of my office building were inspired to allow me this arrangement so that I could get myself established in Los Angeles. Pam and Carl were human angels sent into my life. By supporting my wings to fly, they demonstrated a trust that humbled me.

And fly I did.

I wanted to succeed no matter what it took. I lived this way until I was able to afford my first residence in LA. I felt embarrassed about living in my office and many times withheld that information from some of the new people I met. When asked where I lived, I would give them the name of the neighborhood that my office was located in, but wouldn't be more specific. This would usually suffice for most social conversations.

I feared that people who didn't know me well would judge me negatively. I was having a hard time not judging myself! I was building relationships in a very nontraditional way. I did all this because I had felt an urgency to live part of my life in Los Angeles. I knew that if I waited until I could more easily afford a second residence, I might never make the move. When Spirit awakens a dream within us, there is often an urgency to create it, to fulfill it, and to live it.

I showed up at gatherings looking beautifully put together. People had no idea how much work it took! My rental car served as a mobile closet for my clothing and belongings. I look back on that time now with a smile because I was really pushing myself to make my dream happen.

I was driven by a deeply rooted belief. I knew in the deepest part of me that Los Angeles had something of value for me, and I knew that I had something of value for Los Angeles. I was excited to grow my new community, and I have allowed myself to expand in many exciting ways since those very early days.

Oftentimes the greatest things we have to contribute to this world will only manifest if we are willing to live outside the box of what we think is possible. I was willing to live uncomfortably knowing that I had a place at the table of my dreams. As I sit here now I feel no shame remembering the sacrifices I made for my success. I feel a deep pride and confidence that no one can take away from me. I have developed a steely resilience that has its foundation in the deepest parts of our loving universe.

This resilience is what I desire to awaken and inspire in you as we go through the pages of this book together. I am with you in this process as your partner in accountability. Let's now take a deeper look at what we will be doing to create the changes we want.

Creating the Container for Change

We begin to transform our wounding into strength by:

1. Developing the ability to change the thoughts about what happened both to us and through us
2. Developing the capacity to love, understand, and forgive ourselves
3. Adopting a new lens to view our experiences through so that we may experience more happiness and peace in the present moment
4. Changing the way we create our life experiences as we move forward

Instead of creating from default settings in your mind based on your prior experiences of what you *do not* want, you will begin to create from a more powerful place of intending what you *do* want. This thinking is what attracts to you the people, places, and things you actually want to have in your life. Doing the work of forgiveness is at the foundation of this, for as we know, it's much easier to hold a grudge, or blame others, or fault poor timing for our disappointments. If we choose to hold on to our perspectives that are rooted in our belief of having been wronged by others, or wronged by life in general, we shut down the power available from within us to shift outcomes. We can choose to leave our comfort zone to risk opening up our closed thought system to new ways of perceiving our experiences. This will allow for new options and possibilities to manifest for us. I believe that this type of manifestation is jump-started by the degree to which we are able to live from a heart-centered place of empathy and kindness to whatever degree we are capable of achieving in any given moment. Try making this inner shift as you go about your daily interactions, and see for yourself what begins to happen!

Enlightenment

Throughout each day we make choices to either demonstrate or withhold empathy, compassion, and kindness through our thoughts, words, and actions. When I fully opened to this perspective of healing and was willing to forgive those individuals who had hurt me the most, I experienced what I can best describe as experiences of enlightenment. These individuals actually gifted me with a bird's-eye view into my unresolved core wounding. They also awoke my wounded healer. My own experiences inspired me to investigate the power of this particular healing method, and then to write about it.

At this point I began to read more specifically on the topic of enlightenment. Information seemed to come to me naturally, including the work of Marianne Williamson, American author, spiritual leader, politician, and activist. All of the material that I read by her, lectures of hers that I have attended, and my podcast interview with her I found to be quite powerful, and tremendously helpful in my growth and evolution.

These words from *A Year of Miracles,* by Marianne Williamson, uplifted me and made the experiences of my own inner transformation understandable in words. I offer it to you for consideration: "On Enlightenment—You are loved, and your purpose is to love. From a mind filled with infinite love comes the power to create infinite possibilities. We have the power to think in ways that reflect and attract all the love in the world. Such thinking is called enlightenment. Enlightenment is not a process we work toward, but a choice available to us in any instant."

In contrast, previously, as a problem-solving strategy and a coping mechanism, I'd relied upon the defense mechanism of intellectualization. All my life I depended on the power of my intelligence to cope with loss, grief, betrayal, and other similar challenges. However, over and over again I found that it wasn't enough to understand a situation intellectually to fully heal from it. I discovered that true healing requires invoking forgiveness and compassion as well.

Forgiveness

I have noticed that the word *forgiveness* is overused, while the actual process is underpracticed by many people, myself included. Forgiveness is not a one-time event; forgiveness is a progressively actioned technique. The practice is available *to* us and *for* us, as long as we take breath on this Earth. We will never be beyond the act of forgiving.

I've learned that we need to progressively forgive ourselves, layer by layer, before we can fully forgive another. The embodiment of forgiveness was more of an abstract concept to me—until I had the experience of learning to truly forgive myself. I accomplished this through a concurrent process of forgiving someone who had hurt me deeply.

In the summer of 2014 I found myself in Los Angeles driving to the

LAX airport. I was on my way to pick up a woman whom I'd recently gotten to know through mutual professional associates in New Orleans. It's magical when life puts people together and in this case, she and I had an instant and mutual, energetic resonance. I was led to then share a beautiful portion of my life in LA with her and her great cats. I grew to love her deeply and devoted my energy to creating a relationship with her.

However, she ended things unexpectedly and coldly during a time when I thought we were building a future together.

I couldn't seem to move through the shock, disappointment, and sense of betrayal this engendered in me, no matter how much I wanted to heal from this devastating turn of events. No doubt I'm speaking to some of you who've had this same experience of trying everything you can to move beyond an experience, but you can't. Despite all your efforts, you just can't get *unstuck;* disempowerment can feel like a wet blanket over your head. When she told me that she had deleted the text and email correspondences of our relationship, I became mired in debilitating emotions and physical ailments, stemming from this unexpected and sudden disconnection. Looking back, it was most painful when she said that she had met someone new, someone who was "significant." Having taken the time to be with my inner core wounding, I now know that she was the catalyst for my wounds of Chiron to emerge fully and for me to sit down face-to-face with my own deepest fears of being unimportant, disposable, and unworthy of love. I was left with a jarring sensation of nonexistence. Even as a seasoned healing practitioner, I was paralyzed by feelings that I remember having in childhood, and I felt equally unable to self-soothe as the adult going through this as I once did as a young child. I knew that this loss was unearthing something much bigger than our relationship ending.

When we share a deep intimacy with someone who does not or cannot acknowledge the validity or truth of that intimacy, an energetic disruption may be created, which can precipitate emotional, physical, and spiritual issues. It's important that we handle ourselves with gentle loving care as we heal, and seek the help of professionals when needed, as I did. It is not weak to reach out to others in times of transition and of hardship.

I found myself going round and round in my memory trying to make sense of what I may have missed or misperceived. She and I had just enjoyed an amazing time at my home in New Orleans where we co-created the first live episode of her video podcast. I was so proud to see her shine in her element. Other experiences involved sharing time with my family and friends alongside conversations of committing our lives together as instruments of healing in our shared work. Things fell together effortlessly, and all seemed well.

Over time I had vague flashes and sensations that underneath this loss and the uncertainty ahead of me I had an opportunity to create anew. First, I recognized that I had some deep work to do. I knew that I had to learn to love myself more deeply. However, because my grief was overwhelming, I had no clear idea where to begin, what the work was, or even how to do it.

I realized that I had to forgive myself for the ways that I did not show up for myself. Deciding that I *want* to see this experience differently, I began to understand that my heart had actually been broken open in order to develop the capacity to love more deeply. How many of you have had an experience or two that evoked some of the same feelings I experienced, including the ensuing self-doubt? You might ask yourself some of the following questions: How will I ever trust and love someone again? How can someone do these things and say they love me? What is wrong with me? What is wrong with her, him, them? What do I do now? When faced with the unexpected opening of my core wounding, I immediately defaulted to defense mechanisms of self-protection, rationalizing, bargaining, blaming, and trying to get out and ahead of what had happened. But these and other defense mechanisms I employed simply prolonged my grieving process. It can be hard to differentiate what is right for us and what is good for us. It is especially difficult when words are spoken to us that open our hearts to possibility and hope. Honest and open communication is essential to ensure that we are on the same path as our loved one, or if one of us has taken a turn to explore elsewhere.

Through many dark nights of the soul, I explored my own contribution to the relationship. I had ignored my own inner knowing, and I hadn't used my voice. I learned that when I feel there is a discrepancy between what I am being told and what I feel to be true, I need to check it out, thereby honoring my gut feelings, my intuition, if you will. I had minimized the concerns that had been shown, and in this, I violated my deepest knowing of truth. We can find empowerment in being responsible for our contribution in what we have created. There is healing when we own our part in the co-creation of a situation. We shift from victimhood to warrior/deity/goddess when we claim how we have violated ourselves. There is deep power in self-accountability.

During this time of awakening and healing, I learned to take responsibility for what I did and did not communicate to this particular individual over the course of our relationship. In hindsight I saw that I had defaulted to my (family of origin) patterns of people pleasing, and keeping quiet to maintain the peace, even when I was unhappy. I had given away my power. There is invaluable information available for us when we look at how and when we do not show up for ourselves and, instead, entrust someone else with our happiness and our power. There is a silver lining to be found if we determine that we can and will find it.

Through the development of a meditation practice alongside the necessary emotional work, I learned that I have a beautiful and powerful capacity to love unconditionally. I also came to understand that this individual was a loving person, but one who acted from her hidden core wounds. The truth was that both she and I were wounded in places that complemented our needed growth. In my willingness to look beyond my disappointment, I was able to shift into a powerful inner state of compassion, empathy, forgiveness, and healing.

My shift happened when I came to the place where I decided to try to embody forgiveness, even if this woman might never validate my significance. I released wanting anything from her and, instead, looked inwardly to my own value, worth, beauty, and lovability. In this act of letting go, I freed myself. No one can take from us what we cultivate with unconditional self-love. I appreciate her and the journey we shared, and I am grateful for the life lessons I learned from our time together.

Moving forward, I decided to create for myself the most magnificent life by aligning with the infinite power of the universe. I decided to be happy no matter what. I asked love to sweep through my life and clear out who and what needed to be released in order to prepare me for my best relationship ever. I also asked that Spirit bring that person into my life at the perfect time.

As mentioned earlier, I took a hard and deep look at the contribution I had made in creating the relationship. This opened a hidden door I was able to walk through so that I could progressively heal my heart. From a sincerely loving place of appreciation and deep gratitude, I was eventually able to fully forgive her, and I offered her this prayer: "May you be happy, may you be blessed, and may you be loved."

I said this prayer to myself as well, over and over, allowing myself to receive happiness, blessings, and love with each repetition. As I allowed forgiveness to flow down from my mind into my heart, filling my physical and etheric bodies with acceptance and expansion, I experienced peace of mind and calmness of spirit. I felt that I had awakened myself by going through, layer upon layer, the deep forgiveness necessary to heal my core wounds. I want to let you know that, as I did eventually, you can forgive yourself and heal on your own. Yes, it will be harder, and yes, it will take longer. But you don't need someone else's acknowledgment of your experience to restore yourself to wholeness and sanity.

You are the source of your own power. You can find validation and closure for yourself.

For those of us who, like me, expect a lot from ourselves, we can be our own worse critic. I urge you to release any and all judgment of yourself when you are healing. Acknowledge yourself and trust that you are doing the best that you can from where you are, and that you *will* get stronger and healthier. Following a loss, remind yourself of the core truths of who you are. You are lovable, generous, kind, beautiful, worthy, valuable, and good enough—NOW. Remind yourself that we are here to love and be loved, mutually.

If you are reading this and in a vulnerable place, I want to encourage you to forgive yourself for what has or has not happened. I encourage you to cultivate the deep self-love and compassion for yourself that you deserve.

This is essential for our continued forward movement and momentum in life. It is our birthright to live a joy-centered life—one in which we are safe, seen, and heard. Do not let someone else's wounding rob you of the unconditional love available to you from within your own beating heart.

Forgiving is a progressive and ongoing process. Turn your compassionate heart toward yourself, and say to yourself as often as you can, "I love and forgive you. I am here for you, *no matter what.*" I encourage you to embrace the unlimited potential of your lovability as the person you are right now. This kind of self-forgiveness removes obstacles and is very powerful.

Initiating Change

....

Where the Rubber Meets the Road

To bring enlightenment *through* us we must *feel into* the experience of forgiveness. This process is not something that can be learned by reading a book or following instructions. We usually find that forgiveness comes as a *thought action* while viscerally connecting to the written word, a beautiful view, a loving exchange. In a moment of convergence a simultaneous illumination of mind and energy may be sparked. This convergence awakens enlightenment and can break us open to see where we need to forgive. In this we become the wounded healer who is self-healing. Extrapolated from Joseph Campbell's *The Power of Myth*, apology is a loving act of creation that "opens doors where there were only walls." I encourage you to go to the depths of your inner wounding with empathy and self-forgiveness accompanying you. This opens you to the transformational process of evolution through compassion.

Unconditional Love

Healing and simultaneously being a *healer* through the progressive action of forgiveness is only one embodiment of unconditional love, which also may be experienced as the sharing of a particular moment with our inner being. It can happen while watching a beautiful sunset, being with an infant or a child or the elderly, witnessing an eclipse, being with a pet, hearing beautiful music, feeling into a piece of art, looking deeply into the eyes of another during sexual intimacy, or while looking deeply into your own eyes.

There are as many expressions of unconditional love as there are people. When we permit ourselves to connect with the frequency of unconditional love (of which there is an infinite source), we start to engage with life in a different way.

Commitment

I encourage you to make a contract with yourself right now. Commit to being better at keeping your agreements, and when you can't (or when you change your mind), decide that you will do a better job of letting the other persons who are involved know that you have changed your thinking on the matter. Try this for a month with even the smallest commitment you make, even with those people you think won't remember your commitment or mind when you change it. People do care about what you do or do not deliver on.

Because we are joined through our energetic interconnections, sometimes when we forfeit our contract (word) with others, we may inadvertently wound ourselves with self-criticism. We may hurt others by not showing for them as we had promised we'd do. If you are reading this book, then I know that you're invested in your own well-being as well as the well-being of others. I want to nurture that altruistic part of you so that you can flourish. I want you to learn to nourish that core empathetic self so that you're able to hear the self-forgiving voice of Chiron when he whispers to your frustrations and unmet needs. Greet him with openness and welcome the messages he holds for your fulfillment.

Destruction
and Rebuilding

Enlightenment, forgiveness, unconditional love, and happiness can be experienced in our daily lives if we look for opportunities to *live deeply into the given moments of our lives.* To say that I have lived deeply into every moment of my life would be untrue, for there have been self-indulgent lapses from time to time.

In 2006, the year after Hurricane Katrina, I was an evacuated refugee from New Orleans; my city was underwater, and with thousands of others, I experienced loss that was beyond my capacity to cope with. My family home was flooded; my business was gone; and my family, friends, and clients were dispersed all over the United States. Life as I knew it had been destroyed. I temporarily lost hope and began to live from an unconscious place. I sought pain relief and false happiness by self-medicating with alcohol and drugs. I was miserable and felt as barren and decimated as the city of New Orleans and the Gulf Coast itself.

I reached a crossroads, knowing that I had two simple choices. One option was to continue on as I had been, telling myself that everyone else was in the same boat and doing the same things, so it was *okay* for me to be this way. But I knew inwardly that I was becoming increasingly depleted, erratic, isolated, and, underneath my outward appearance, very unhappy. I began to physically, emotionally, and spiritually approach a cliff, which some part of me knew could lead to my death if unaddressed.

Addiction wants to be our primary attachment, and it wants an exclusive relationship with us. We may find some desired temporary distractions, but a continual avoidance of issues that we consciously need to examine eventually leads to a painful malaise of body, mind, and heart, and a degrading of social and spiritual connections.

My second option was to stop living incongruously and begin the practical steps necessary to change the people, places, and things that were in any way related to my maladaptive self-care. I began to reconstruct my life. I decided to rebuild myself in such a way that I would be stronger than I had been before Katrina hit. To transform the areas of emotional wounding that my addictive behaviors and maladaptive coping patterns had tried to protect me from addressing, I reentered therapy to explore the underlying roots of my pain and correlating self-sabotaging addictive behaviors. I became responsible for myself, and *most importantly*, I was willing to change.

At that time a book fell into my lap. Entitled *Racing for Recovery: From Addict to Ironman,* Todd Crandell's book intrigued me. Being a fitness instructor (cyclist), I found that his methods for recovery through participation in the Ironman triathlons intuitively spoke to me.

I began to train for a triathlon, and I eventually completed three Ironman 70.3-mile triathlons! During this time I met a professional Ironman 140.6-mile triathlete trainer, Amy, while on a beach vacation in Pensacola, Florida. We became friends, and I began to spend some of my weekends in Pensacola swimming, surfing, and running.

Amy reinspired me to dig deeply within myself and identify what mattered to me at this juncture of my life. By being willing to release old habits and replace them with new and healthy ones, I was able to quickly shift the direction of my life so that it was on a positive trajectory.

The wounded healer within me began to transform from the ground up. As a result, from that time forward I developed open-hearted empathy for people who struggle with addictive thoughts, habits, and behaviors. I am able to offer creative solutions to my clients as a result of my own healing. I share my personal story with you as an example and a reminder that you, too, can change and heal, no matter what.

Boundaries

In learning to adopt healthy ways to cope, I began to progressively practice setting boundaries with others, which took some trial and error.
As women we are raised and encouraged to meet the needs of others,
and our culture maintains and reinforces this expectation of "woman as
nurturer." This belief certainly showed up powerfully in my life, especially in the realm of intimate relationships.

Chiron encourages us to set necessary boundaries and draw lines
in the sand to let people know how they may enter the arenas of our
lives and where they cannot cross. It is an empowering process to take
responsibility for our own happiness. And it's life enhancing to adopt
belief systems and behaviors that are in alignment with one's core values.

I wonder if some of you reading might want to develop greater proficiency in learning how to show up for yourself in intimate relationships. You can redefine the way you want to experience intimacy in your
life and begin to show up for yourself in ways that support your vision.
As you begin to consistently take a stand for yourself, I want you to
know that life itself will meet you in that space of co-creation. People,
places, and things will align in perfect harmony for you.

The Seasons of Life

I encourage you to be willing to see people and things through the
eyes of your heart instead of your ego mind. Once you perceive the
truth of a person or situation, I encourage you and your behavior
toward that person or situation to shift and change accordingly. I
haven't made these shifts and changes seamlessly. What I *have* found,
and offer to you, is that as time moves onward we can become more
skilled at looking ahead for triggering events and environments. At
this point in my life I do not go to certain events or places that I
know will be unhealthy for me. Instead, I look for opportunities that

will add supportive people, places, and experiences to my life, *and* that are in alignment with my goals.

I suggest that you periodically evaluate the various areas of your life to see if they currently fit and serve to nurture your growth and evolution. I've developed practices that help me be mindful in public environments and with the people I'm surrounded by. I have evolved into being more mindful in social situations and filling some of my quiet times with meditation, writing, and reading. It can be helpful to use the quieter times of introspection as gifts to care for and nurture oneself.

I've taken a risk by revealing my personal inner struggles with you. As the reader, of course, you may judge me. I am willing to be vulnerable because in my transparency you become my accountability partner. We enlist others to support our recovery and healing when we verbalize our desire for it. I've learned that the hardships we overcome become the source of our greatest successes. You may see in my story aspects of your own shadow selves or misguided attempts to cope. Reveal yourself to others so that they may become your partners in healing.

I trust that you want to be seen, heard, validated, loved, respected, and valued. These are some of the deepest needs of humanity. Unfortunately, we often find the fulfillment of those needs sabotaged by Chiron's unhealed core wounding. Together let's work on healing these wounds.

The Stages of Change

In making changes in yourself and in your life it's important to know that the path to wholeness is often nonlinear. When we decide to visit and heal our core wounds we engage in stages of decision making that we navigate with our thoughts. And our thoughts are not linear, are they?

While contemplating this section of the book, I was reminded of a model of decision making called the Transtheoretical Model (TTM), which pertains to the way we approach making changes in our lives. We tend to go through these stages intuitively and naturally. Here I will outline the three-step process of the TTM of change. The first stage is called precontemplation. This is where we notice others who are living in a manner we aspire to and seek to emulate. In our precontemplation, we may ask them how they got to where they are. Or we may research information about the changes they have made that we are seeking to make in our own lives. These changes may include such things as assessing abstaining from drugs and alcohol, taking up the practice of meditation, or becoming vegetarian/vegan, for instance.

Once we find the information we are looking for, we can determine a path of change. At this point we internally commit at a higher level, which is the second stage of change and one that is termed *contemplation*. In this stage we begin to analyze what situations we would encounter if we were to make the changes we are considering. Here's an example: If we are either curtailing our use of alcohol or abstaining from alcohol altogether, what would that actually look like for us at a dinner party with friends? Or in the setting of a business cocktail hour, when on a date, or out with familiar friends at happy hour?. How would we handle those occasions, and what would we tell people? Would we order a mocktail? How uncomfortable would we feel at this stage of our process?

Other examples: If we decide that getting in better shape physically is in order, we can begin to think about what gym we might join and how to schedule our workouts, or what foods we might stop eating if we decide to live life as vegetarian/vegan. In this case the question becomes: What foods could we eat instead of meat? When we begin to imagine our lives through the various lenses of our proposed change, we can *feel into* how it would be for us to actually take those steps.

The third stage of the TTM of change is called implementation. This is when we take action. We go and sign the contract at the gym, we purchase vegetarian/vegan food items in lieu of meat, or we say no to alcohol or drugs. We take action to develop a support system to sustain our decisions.

Oftentimes in making a major change in our lives we may vacillate between the contemplation and implementation stages over and over again. This is akin to learning to ride a bike wherein we often fall time and again during the learning process. This vacillation doesn't necessarily mean we have failed in our attempts to effect change in our lives. When we begin to restructure our identity we try on alternatives. In this we create new neural pathways in the brain, and patience is called for.

Without harsh judgments of yourself, allow yourself to explore this space in between the old and the new. Try to have realistic expectations and implement your strategy of change with small baby step goals. Be available in the continuous present to listen to your inner voice for direction. This voice will become easier to identify and follow over time. I found that my inner voice was easier to detect through the resonance of the heart instead of the chatter of the mind. Tuning into the eyes of one's heart will strengthen one's connection to the empathetic healer within.

As a result of doing our inner work, we can find happiness in the smallest of things. You may decide to pause to smell fresh flowers on your walk, listen to the birds singing in the trees, or run on the beach without music to hear the sound of the waves washing ashore. Life will begin to take on a quietness and peace that you weren't conscious of before.

Hyperarousal and Hypervigilance

If you grew up in a home where there was inconsistency due to emotional, physical, or sexual abuse, or other violence or neglect—or the witnessing of emotional, physical, or sexual abuse, violence, neglect—no doubt you were physiologically in a consistent state of hyperarousal and hypervigilance.

This means that your central nervous system (CNS) is, as an adult, in physiological hyperalert at all times. As a result, you may continuously, consciously or subconsciously, scan the environment for emotional, physical, or sexual danger, unpredictability, or chaos. Being hyperalert means that you never fully trust that the moments of quiet and peace that you do experience will be other than fleeting.

You therefore find yourself in a perpetual state of waiting for the other shoe to drop, which it always does at some point. And when it does, you are cast back into neurological distress often without an appropriate context of comfort or care. This hypervigilance is a normal reaction to the abnormal experiences of chaos, abuse, trauma, unpredictability, uncertainty, and fear.

As survivors of trauma we may naturally default to an array of self-protective mechanisms of defense, including dissociation, depersonalization, intellectualization, sublimation, repression, denial, reaction formation, compartmentalization, projection, or acting out. To mediate our pain and meet our needs, these compensatory methods saved us from absorbing the stressful reality of what was happening in our lives at the time.

As we grow into adulthood these defensive mechanisms turn against us and become maladaptive. They cause us problems with our affect regulation (i.e., emotional balance) and in our relationships with others.

As adults many of us succeed in creating a life of sustained peace and tranquility, and yet at the same time we may encounter emotional triggers, which provoke us into worrying that something intrusive or negative may come along to take away what we have.

A trigger is an unhealed memory or energetic attachment lying dormant, waiting to be discovered, akin to stepping on a hidden land mine. Triggers often reside in the shadows and hidden recesses of our consciousness and may be completely out of our normal everyday awareness.

It's important to reassure yourself during and after having been triggered that you are having a natural reaction to a wound that has been hidden from your consciousness. You may be experiencing a reaction to core wounding that has been opened up and activated. It has made its presence known to you so that you can embrace the parts of yourself that Chiron illuminates.

As a young person it may be that you didn't have the power to create or maintain peace in your environment no matter how hard you tried. Where you stand now, as an adult, is different. Once you begin to apply daily empathy and self-forgiveness to the vulnerabilities that Chiron reveals, no one will have the power to take away the confidence you're building. You will experience a new way of living life that is progressively filled with what you want and contains less and less of what you don't want.

The more often you give yourself permission to experience inner peace, joy, happiness, love, and bliss, the more deeply you rewire the neural pathways of your brain to adapt to a new baseline of existence that's rooted in stability. You can begin to feel safe as you gradually bring yourself into interior alignment with your core self. There will be fewer and fewer experiences of disappointment and hardship to navigate because you have changed your patterns.

Externalizing Our Triggers

When you feel aroused in a negative way you can choose to externalize your reaction by temporarily taking an objective stance from the place of your inner observer. This is different from dissociating because using your inner observer is a construct of a learned skill and technique that helps you accurately identify a potentially triggering emotional exchange.

It may help you to visualize the other person's emotions as a color or shape so that you can imagine blocking them, putting them in a box, walking the emotions out your front door, sending them out of a window, asking them to leave, or sealing yourself in love and light. It may also help you to name that annoying aspect of the person who is triggering you. You can choose to refer to it as that person's alter ego, ten-year-old self, or your favorite nickname in order to bring some humor to the situation. These are mental/psychological techniques to take the power and emotional charge out of challenging interpersonal interactions.

I think that when our triggers erupt, the associated emotions that we feel often are so intense that we instinctively believe they have power over us, and then, of course, we fear being emotionally out of control. By using the techniques I suggest above, we can interrupt the process of escalation and allow the emotional charge of the triggered feelings to subside.

I suggest that you take a private moment of quiet time when you feel yourself in a personal interaction with someone and you're respond-ing to an emotion that they have triggered within you. In that moment, inwardly promise yourself that you'll attend to that part of your inner world later on in a private moment when you can look at it more closely and work through what's coming up. I inwardly talk to myself in this way to self-soothe. A seemingly powerful emotion can fall away with the gentle commitment to properly address it later. This is what it means to consciously stay present. This is mindfulness in action.

The resulting insights we are left with following a trigger allow us to see more clearly with the inner eyes of our heart. For it's our heart that mediates between our instinctual impulses of sexuality and aggres-sion (lower chakras) and the higher executive functioning of our upper chakras.

Our thoughts and perceptions precede our actions. It's the reason that more of what is thought about actually comes about. This works well for us if we are in alignment with healthy and positive influences, and if we are creating from a place where we feel abundant, grateful, joyful, and secure. To sustain our lives from this powerful vantage point it's important to take the time and make the effort to identify and heal our core wounding.

Transformation

In order to be used in service to our happiness, our wounds want to be taken out into the light of day so that they may be fully seen, heard, understood, transformed, and integrated. Embrace the ideas and insights contained in this book. Dismantle thought systems that are based in fear, and replace them with thought systems based in love.

Through the application of self-forgiveness and empathy, this shift in consciousness becomes the transformation of your core wounding. In flashes of insight and deeper love for others and yourself, you will begin to see situations and problems differently because you've been willing to view them from an alternative vantage point.

In traditional psychotherapy and psychology this is called reframing or making a paradigm shift. In this way we can shift into an existence of enhanced peace, joy, contentment, and happiness. This skill is essential in moving through and then making meaning from the pain of the past.

I have used the teachings of Louise Hay, one of my favorite authors and visionaries, to reshape my belief systems. I want to share an excerpt from her book, *The Power Is Within You,* that may be helpful to you:

Life is a voyage of self-discovery. To me, to be enlightened is to go within and to know who and what we really are, and to know that we have the ability to change for the better by loving and taking care of ourselves. . . . When I talk about loving ourselves, I mean having a deep appreciation for who we are. We accept all the different parts of ourselves—our little peculiarities, the embarrassments, the things we may not do so well, and all the wonderful qualities, too. . . . We often put conditions on our love. But we can change. We can love ourselves as we are right now!

With understanding, self-forgiveness, and empathy, I encourage you to consider accepting yourself just as you are right now, in this very moment.

3

The Power of Your Mind

Responding as opposed to *reacting* requires that we develop skills and tools that allow us to consistently interrupt the thinking patterns that have led us to engage in unwanted behaviors. One such tool is the development of what's called somatic screening skills to interpret, decode, and intervene in the emotional escalation system that is activated in the neural pathways of our brain.

The brain and central nervous system (CNS) are able to instantaneously accumulate and interpret all previously encoded memories that appear to be similar to the current stimuli being received. This two-part process happens in nanoseconds, after which we are sent messages for further engagement.

The internal meanings we then create are based on our sensory perceptions. As is stated in that classic text *A Course in Miracles,* "The world we see merely reflects our own internal frame of reference—the dominant ideas, wishes and emotions in our minds. 'Projection makes perception.' . . . As a man thinks, so does he perceive. Therefore, seek not to change the world, but choose to change your mind about the world. Perception is a result and not a cause."

One way to develop a somatic screening skill is as easy as breathing. Literally. We can choose to actively slow down our reactive emotional system by using our breath. Before reacting and responding, try taking some slow, deep, thoughtful breaths. This will buy you some time to decode the information you are receiving during what may be a tense interaction. This is an important skill to use when engaging in controversial and heated topics with family members, or with intimate partners, telemarketers, solicitors, and friends. These are some of the people we are most often triggered by!

We can also be triggered by our own mind when we are alone. How many times have you imagined or fantasized a dialogue with someone when there may be bothersome unfinished business between you? To defend feeling angry and resentful we might imagine entire exchanges in our mind that will probably not transpire in real life. Or we might imagine a conversation that transpired years ago, and in the present moment, we find ourselves with raised blood pressure, sweaty palms, shallow breathing, and agitated mannerisms, all of which may culminate in huffing and puffing around a room when there is no one there but us! We can go from being peaceful and calm to raging with anger or experiencing deep sadness in a matter of seconds by just thinking about things that happened years ago, or things that have not yet happened!

Cultivating Curiosity about Our Defensiveness

The mind is a powerful tool that is remarkable in its abilities to imagine and create. Let's join in an intention to be slow to anger with each other and instead respond with curiosity and calmness. Instead of responding in defensiveness, let's uncover more information with the intention of mutual understanding and resolution.

It is easier to interrupt a potential emotional escalation in the early stages of dialogue than in later stages when one person or the other may bring up unresolved situations from the past to add fuel to their perspective. Instead of reacting, it's important to give yourself permission to take the time needed to slow down and think about how you want to respond. Often it's the case that we attack ourselves for our shortcomings as well as identify flaws in others. In that light, I ask you to consider this perspective from *A Course in Miracles*, "The only thing that is required for healing is a lack of fear. . . . This does not mean the conflict must be gone forever from your mind to heal. For if it were, there would be no need for healing then. But it does mean, if only for an *instant*, you love without attack."

Sometimes we may not know exactly what we are feeling (or why) in the moment of an interaction. We may feel an "ouch," or a sense that something isn't right. It's appropriate to hold on to that information until a future time. We also might need to step away from the situation in order to gain mental and emotional clarity.

Allow yourself to step back and process things from a place of inner peace and clarity. As a result of practicing self-restraint and temperance, you'll feel good about yourself in the long term. Let's also make an agreement with our loved ones to help each other communicate in this fashion. When Chiron's core wounds are triggered, I offer you the meditation below for self-soothing.

❧ Guided Visualization for Healing

First take a deep breath in through the nose and blow it audibly out of your mouth. Ahhh . . . . *Let's do this again: in through the nose and forcefully out through the mouth, removing all the stale air from your lungs.*

Now begin to breathe regularly so that you are comfortable. Envision in your mind a space free of all thoughts and responsibilities. It may be outside in the open air, a clear space of green grass, an expansive beach of white sand, the open ocean, a large white room, or wherever your own imagination takes you.

Imagine yourself in the center of this expansive and clear space that is rich with clean, fresh nurturing air and vibrant energy. With each breath you inhale you are literally cleaning your body, mind, and spirit, right down to the molecules of your DNA. As you breathe in and out, only peace and unconditional love exist in this space for you.

Envision living in this spaciousness of energy every day and at every moment of your life. This is your cleared space of healing, and with every deep, gathering breath, your inner being is filling with light, and every cell is repeatedly being filled with exactly what you need in this place and at this time. Stay in this place as long as is needed to completely relax. With each exhale, let go of everything that may be troubling you.

When you're ready, thank this energy for filling your mind, body, and spirit with healing, and then thank yourself for taking the time to be joined with this guiding presence of unconditional love that is always available to you.

Before leaving this meditation, if you notice yourself being distracted by an unresolved situation with someone, take a few moments and call to mind this person who has disrupted you, and couple their presence with a deepened awareness of how much love they need to feel whole, complete, and happy.

It helps to imagine them as the little child they once were, and to acknowledge that they too were wounded deeply and needed to be loved more than they were at that time. These individuals are not evil; they are broken in tender places of vulnerability. Send them love now.

Finally, say out loud, "Thank you for my inner peace; may it pervade every area of my life and the lives of those I love." Take a few centering breaths, and gently come back into the room you're in.

All minds are joined, and we are one human species. As you love others, you're receiving love yourself. Bright white healing energy is magnified within you and bringing you closer and closer to all that you want and need to be whole, happy, and at peace.

When you see with your inner eye the connection we all share with each other, your emotions may be able to soften toward those you have been in conflict with, including your inner self.

I partner with you in this co-creation. May it be a powerful manifestation tool of reconciliation and love for you. And so it is, and so it shall be, in every direction, and in all dimensions of time, Amen.

Up to Seventy Thousand Thoughts a Day!

It is impossible to monitor every thought that crosses one's mind. It is also impossible to engage in the mental gymnastics required to shift each and every thought in a positive direction. How do we approach this task without even a template or road map to use as a guide?

A favorite mentor and friend of mine is the author, life coach, and mindfulness meditation teacher Ora Nadrich. She has created a model that has helped many people (including me) shift our self-defeating thoughts by asking ourselves a series of questions when we feel an emotional disruption. Her self-discovery process helps us to dismantle our reactive emotional response system, question by question.

In her book *Says Who? How One Simple Question Can Change the Way You Think Forever*, Nadrich teaches the method of how to release negative and fear-based thoughts and replace them with loving thoughts that support us. Her process is based on the premise that "many of the obstacles people face are the result of their own negative thoughts holding them back. And often those thoughts don't even originate within them; they're the ideas or opinions of someone else—a critical parent or angry spouse, for instance—which they believe without questioning to see if they're even real or true. Since thoughts create beliefs—which then create behavior—negative thoughts are dangerous things to leave unchecked. You must question them, challenge them."

What Nadrich's method highlights is the importance of taking ownership for our healing. Understanding our portion of responsibility in any given situation holds the potential for resolution and frees us up so that we don't repeat that experience again. *New York Times* best-selling author, dear mentor, and friend Katherine Woodward Thomas articulates "responsibility as power" when she invites us to ask ourselves how we are the source of our experiences. This question, honestly addressed, restores power to our own selves and helps us learn from our mistakes. Here is a set of powerful questions she poses to the reader in *Calling in "The One": 7 Weeks to Attract the Love of Your Life,* "How is it happening *through* you, and not just *to* you? Who do we need to become to fulfill the intentions we set? What do we need to let go of, and what do we need to embrace?"

It is instinctual to blame the other person, who we feel is primarily responsible for the dissolution of a relationship we'd once cherished. We assess blame because, after all, they fell out of love; or met someone else, changed their mind, lied to us, or betrayed our trust; or abandoned us, stole from us, or hurt us. But what is most important to focus on now is our contribution to the situation, no matter how small we think it is or was.

Chiron holds clues to that portion of our responsibility that is contributing to the unhappiness we feel. Your situation may involve feeling neglected emotionally or physically despite your best efforts to not feel this way. Or due to a damaged sense of self-worth and value, you may be living below your financial potential. Or perhaps you are staying with a partner who neglects your deepest needs because you fear he or she will abandon you. You may not be recognized for your contributions at work, or in your family; you may feel uncertain about how to create and maintain a stable home environment; you may feel cut off from your creativity and passion; or you may neglect your own health. Other aspects of Chiron's core wounding may point to a profound inability to be alone, meaning you may compulsively pursue relationships even if they are clearly neither healthy nor satisfying.

Misaligned Power and Disconnection

As emphasized, Chiron's untreated core wounding can lead to a host of challenges and difficulties. Here is an abbreviated list of examples:

1. You may have been wounded from someone's misaligned sense of power, and because of this you may manipulate others as a way to feel in control.
2. You may sabotage yourself by undervaluing your worth.
3. You may neglect your own health and incur serious problems as a result.
4. You may feel disconnected and isolated from your peers and social connections while longing to be a part of them.
5. You may have been neglected, and experience a painful lack of connection to others, making it hard to believe that you can be secure and safe in the world.
6. You may falsely believe that you are insignificant.
7. You may find yourself stuck in patterns of blame, shame, and self-loathing and feel that you lack the inner resources to change.
8. You may have an addiction, or addictive behaviors, including to alcohol or drugs (prescription or street), sex, food (restriction and overeating), hoarding, exercise, or shopping.
9. You may have cut yourself off from your own creativity and inner happiness.
10. You may have experienced a series of dead-end relationships.
11. You may be experiencing financial struggle.
12. You may lack sought-after professional success.

All of these conditions are treatable. If we are willing to strip down our insides to our authentic base needs and related emotions, we will be able to get real with ourselves. We all have negative, angry, and self-defeating thoughts. That's okay. Let's give ourselves permission to be honest with ourselves *about* our thoughts and choose to work *with* them, especially when we find ourselves motivated by fear, jealousy, revenge, anger, sadness, loss, helplessness, despair, or hatred. Left buried, our unacknowledged emotions cause us to act in ways that sabotage us and to display behaviors that damage the people, places, and things we care about. When we acknowledge these thoughts and desires within ourselves—then ask them to be transformed and follow up with the real work of transformation—our thoughts, words, and actions begin to shift. From this grounded stance of personal honesty we begin to show up for ourselves in new ways. We begin to speak differently with others as we create new outcomes that promote mutual connection. Finally, we generate power sourced directly from the transformation of our core wounds.

Don't You Have *Your* Shit Together?!?

I work with many healing professionals who turn to me for help with their own dysfunctional patterns or because they feel stuck in their own lives and are not sure what to do. I have been there myself. Whenever I hear this I perceive an undercurrent of self-blame and shame. As a reader you may be a healing professional who is struggling. There is an unspoken expectation in our line of work that we are supposed to "have it all together." In case you didn't get the memo (which I received years ago), let me break this to you: None of us are perfect! We are all fleshy humans with biological, psychological, social, spiritual, sexual, and physical vulnerabilities that may get in our way—and that's *okay.* As long as we're moving toward self-accountability for ourselves and evolving up through our self-care practices, we will maintain the alignment necessary to work with the pain of others within a framework of integrity.

Today I find acceptance for my imperfections. I have been able to extend this compassionate understanding to others in my life as a result of accurately empathizing with myself and employing self-forgiveness.

I metaphorically represent the process of self-forgiveness through art by repurposing found objects in much of my sculpture and collage work. What that really means is that I use other people's garbage to create complex assemblages utilizing discarded pieces of steel, aluminum, wood, glass, and so on. I go to scrapyards and pick up debris left on the streets.

You can't buy new that which time has weathered into beauty. As humans we are the same. I value our rusted and worn parts. And I love conversing about our collective journey in becoming. For that reason I started my podcast, *All Things Therapy,* in 2016. The show gives me a wonderful public platform to ask people how they came to be the person they are, and I get to share those same bits and pieces about myself. The differences between us lend us texture and contrast. Instead of ignoring, numbing from, projecting onto, blaming, dismissing, judging, dissociating from, or criticizing ourselves and faulting others, let's unpack our past with patience and compassion. Let's look at the gifts inherent in the opportunity we have in healing our core wounds. Let's seek to uncover the beauty hidden.

Spiritual Bypass

The inner disconnection from our core wounded self fuels our confusion about knowing how to cope with and soothe these wounds when they erupt. We may be in need of help and unsure where and whom to turn to. A broader perspective of this confusion we feel can be traced to the consumerization of psychology, spirituality, and healing.

One example of this would be practitioners who offer services utilizing an *aspect* of authentic psychology and spirituality, which is then presented as a quick fix for what are often very *deep* emotional wounds. This is pushed onto individuals in our culture who truly have a genuine hunger for reliable ways to transition out of pain and into joy. Examples of spiritual bypass include services offered for what may typically be, on average, a very high cost by a practitioner with little or no actual professional training in working with the pain of others. Be sure to check the education and training, credentials, and experience of a healing practitioner, especially if you are a survivor of trauma, loss, grief, or addictions. It should be said that to facilitate effectively the healing of emotional and spiritual suffering requires that the practitioner have both a proficient knowledge base from which to draw and an emotional sensitivity to the experiences of the client.

I think that by doing our own inner work consistently we professionals can deliver services that support our clients in their healing so they do not become overly dependent on us as their only hope. I have heard of practitioners who foster dependency from their clients by claiming to be the *only* intuitive channel for them. The truth is that *you* are your *own* intuitive channel! You can work with professionals to develop and enhance your own connection to that Source within you, but remember that *you* are your Source, and *you* can learn to tune in and hear the whisper of *your* deep inner knowing. You absolutely can.

Robert Augustus Masters, Ph.D., in his book *Spiritual Bypassing: When Spirituality Disconnects Us from What Really Matters* makes this powerful statement on spiritual bypass:

Getting more intimate with our "lower" qualities—all those things that we may think we should be transcending—is not a particularly popular topic for those of us enamored with spiritual bypassing. In fact, it's such a downer that it's usually only handled with spiritual tongs, lifted and dropped into sterilized vats brimming with affirmations, meditational tranquility, and other uplifting strategies, as if there's nothing to be done with the "lower" other than converting it to something "higher" (much like indigenous tribes in the hands of European missionaries). Healing is a circuitous path often taking everything that one has to navigate the road less traveled, overgrown with obscured branches, vines, and hidden vermin, making each step tedious and unknown upon what type of landing one's foot will be met with underneath: quicksand, water, a steel trap, or soft grass and safety on higher ground.

In contrast to spiritual bypass are the foundational truths present not only in this book, but also in the work of many others, some of whom are referenced at the end of this book in the resources section. There you will find a list of providers, websites, books, and general information to utilize. The list is not exhaustive, but it is a compilation of sources that I value. My goal is to empower you to transform your life through self-healing. I invite you to dive deeply into your mind to explore what lies beneath its surface.

The Shadow

What really matters is not so much the presence of our shadow side as the kind of relationship we choose to have with it. In spiritual bypass we choose either to have no relationship with our dark impulses or to cultivate only an intellectual relationship with them. Either way, it's easy to see how we can keep our shadow world in the darkness of our unconscious.

Deepak Chopra says in *Super Brain: Unleashing the Explosive Power of Your Mind to Maximize Health, Happiness, and Spiritual Well-Being,*

How easy and how commonplace it is to turn away from what we don't like about ourselves, housing it so far below the surface that its cries cannot be heard, except perhaps as a distant echo. And yes its fists, its often tiny and so very young fists, continue hammering against the inside of our chest, calling to us, calling for us, calling for connection, illumination, love, and healing. All we have to do is enter what we have spent most of our life trying to escape or deny— a tall order, yes, but one that is definitely possible to achieve, step by conscious step.

Let's journey together to the depths of our hidden inner truths. Let's allow Chiron to lead us to the waters of self-forgiveness through empathy. Our dreams are what await us in a state of gestation, ready to be birthed as the beautiful and powerful wounded healer within.

4

The Foundation

....
Emotional Safety and Gratitude

A prerequisite for the healing work that we will undertake with psychoastrology is that you create an emotionally safe place from which to venture forth into the work itself. You are embarking on a journey into your past to explore your wounds and resulting areas of vulnerability. The holding of this emotionally safe place may entail setting aside a specific time and space to do this introspective work. You may also consider lining up a trusted individual/professional to speak with during this process and procure a journal in which to document the insights and patterns that will emerge for you during this time.

Employ empathy, love, and forgiveness while you work on your memories of being wounded. This will soften the experience and aid in your healing. I like the way the Fourteenth Dalai Lama speaks of our ability to hold space for one another when he says, "Our innate capacity for empathy is the source of the most precious of all human qualities."

Empathy and Intuition

All of the placements of Chiron may invoke empathy within us and amplify our intuitive abilities to enhance our ability to shift our thoughts and beliefs in order to heal our lives. This is why it's so important to honor one's intuition. "Intuition is a spiritual faculty and does not explain but simply points the way," said Florence Scovel Shinn, New Thought spiritual teacher and metaphysical writer of the late 1800s. I encourage you to embrace your own intuition as your innate ability to understand something immediately, without the need for conscious reasoning.

Empathy is defined as the ability to understand and share the feelings and experiences of another person. Practices that teach us to view ourselves through a lens of forgiveness engender empathy and will bring long-lasting peace and happiness to our lives.

Judgment

As an artist and therapist, and one who is a seeker, I have been taught to look for the weak links in a system in order to offer a plan to correct and support it. But there is a shadow side to having such an analytical perception. The vision and willingness it takes to see untapped potential in others means that what might arise is the propensity to criticize others when they are not living up to their potential. At the very same time, we often judge ourselves harshly when we forget that we are works in progress too. Instead we deserve to love ourselves as the beautifully flawed humans that we are.

I actively work to encourage my clients to heal core wounding through the eyes of love and compassion, instead of criticism and judgment. My hope is that this book inspires you to do your personal healing work. As you begin this work, it is also my hope that you come to understand the priceless value of choosing to be a catalyst of change to promote energetic healing at a global level. As we journey on our individual paths we support healing for the collective.

Every time we take responsibility for our words and actions and make amends for our wrongs, an energetic and etheric shift ripples across the entire world and reaches people we will never meet or know. When we heal ourselves, we model permission for others to do the same.

It is my passion to educate and inspire by revealing some of my own experiences to you. When working with psychoastrology, here are some things I consistently remind myself, and I ask you to do the same. Each time painful memories arise within you:

1. Do have respect for your feelings while being gentle and patient with yourself in this process of discovery.
2. Do commit to trust, and believe that you can heal.
3. Do believe that you can shift from fear as your motivator to love as your motivator.
4. Take a quiet moment each morning to remind yourself to honor and respect yourself today.
5. Remind yourself to praise yourself throughout your day—no matter what happens. You can say things to yourself such as, "I'm doing really well," "I love who I am," or "I am making great decisions." This foundation will facilitate the creation of a safe emotional space in which you may contain your work of complete self-forgiveness.

Trauma and Recovery

Early on in my psychotherapy career I was exposed to the work of Dr. Judith Herman and her book *Trauma and Recovery*. She outlines a three-stage model of healing for survivors of trauma, violence, and abuse consisting of:

1. Safety
2. Remembrance
3. Reconnection

Traumatic experiences may have caused us to fragment and separate from our own inner knowing of people, places, and things. Therefore, reconnection to these compartments of our lives is key to our healing. As Dr. Herman says in her book, "Because the core experiences of psychological trauma are disempowerment and disconnection from others, recovery is based on the empowerment of the survivor and the creation of new connections."

Because disconnection and fragmentation are at the center of our core wounds, I work with my clients to develop mindfulness practices that consist of dedicated periods of time for inner reflection, paired with actively replacing and shifting judgmental and critical thoughts. This practice facilitates the development of seeing oneself from the perspective of an *observer*. This subject/object differentiation aids in viewing experiences of core wounding from a new vantage point. The observer's psychological vantage point affords just the growth edge we need to not take things so personally. Viewing ourselves from various vantage points can immediately shift feelings of regret, anger, depression, and anxiety. We can depersonalize experiences of wounding in this way and see them instead as information that is being offered to us. We are able to separate from the powerful feelings created by judging and blaming ourselves. We can contain our emotions in this space of neutrality. We can then begin to step into forgiveness and remediate any negative feelings we have toward ourselves.

The Voice in Your Head

There exists a false cultural belief that people only change as a result of harsh criticism and punishment. Yet another false belief suggests that if we forgive ourselves, then we may end up giving ourselves permission to be lazy and complacent. Both are incorrect. I have personally experienced, and seen in others, healing that takes hold more quickly and with longer-lasting results through the practice of compassion, understanding, and forgiveness.

We can learn to speak to ourselves through our self-talk, with the voice of a loving and inspiring coach who believes in us, as opposed to a default, self-same cruel and punishing taskmaster. The practice of either self-encouragement or self-deprecation literally shapes what we will experience in our future.

Impregnate your future with possibility instead of limitation and watch the effects of our thoughts naturally begin to remediate as we shift the influences that underlie them. Just like going to the gym to train our muscles by lifting weights, to train the attitudinal muscles of our mind we can choose to draw upon the therapeutic powers of meditation, prayer, yoga, writing in a journal, being out in nature, or reading a book, for example.

Whatever you plant in your body and mind will grow. I believe in the cultivation of body and mind through energetically enhancing healthy experiences that fully absorb one in the moment. Activities and practices that involve tapping into one's passion and creativity are the most powerful and effective. Peak experiences are as vast as the ocean itself, so allow yourself to feel into this process and decide what works for you.

There are infinite paths to take in the journey to finding one's pleasures and passions. Remember that we always have an inner guidance system to rely on. It will invariably inform us about our desires—whether or not they are healthy or unhealthy, or if they might cause harm to another or to ourselves.

When we are in alignment with ourselves, our inner navigation system works harmoniously to chart our course in the flow of life. This alignment is found when we are being loving and kind to ourselves, and liking the person we truly are. We also tend to treat others better as a natural outgrowth of our self-respect and care.

The moral compass of our personality can become murky, even obscured, by our unconscious core wounds. We are prone to act in ways that may be highly unlike ourselves and then feel shame as a result. Our unconscious needs keep us from considering all of the factors when making important decisions in our lives. Our growth is dependent on giving ourselves permission to try new things while at the same time encouraging ourselves to be respectful in the fulfillment of our pleasures.

Internal versus External Drivers

Let's look at internal versus external drivers of pleasure and the influence they have on our behaviors. Take a moment right now to get a paper and pen and write down all of the ways you can think of to experience pleasure.

Some of the most common *internally* derived sources of pleasure available to us are through laughter, being generous, finding deeper meaning/purpose, being creative, spirituality, expressing kindness, knowing your worth and value, feeling successful, being of service, self-validation, and so on.

Some of the most common *externally* derived sources of pleasure available to us are sexual exploration and gratification, time spent with friends and family, interacting with pets, traveling, exploring nature, going off on adventures, going on vacation, spending money, drinking alcohol, taking drugs, going shopping, volunteering, baking and cooking and eating, working out, being creative, playing or listening to music, indulging in the arts, watching movies, going to the theater, acting, or writing.

Notice how many items on your list consist of experiences derived from internal sources of pleasure versus external sources of pleasure.

Is your list skewed toward externally derived pleasures rather than internally derived pleasures? A lot of us, me included, derive pleasure and well-being from externally derived sources because typically they are more accessible. We are housed in a body, and the body likes to feel good.

It's common knowledge that pleasurable effects from externally derived sources are sometimes shorter lasting, even fleeting. Often we are left with a gnawing emptiness that has not been filled or satiated. If we are looking for healthy balance, it's productive to find compensatory self-care practices that are inwardly sourced, such as meditation or a spiritual practice. It's important that we source pleasure from both internally and externally derived methods in order to live happily, in balance, and with contentment. Having a sense of meaning and purpose is highly correlated with the inner fulfillment we desire. Your early life experiences pertaining to how empathetically attuned your caregivers were to your needs is a factor in your capacity to develop empathy. The reader who takes pleasure regardless of how it affects others has an underdeveloped sense of empathy. In contrast, some of you may restrict your pleasure due to an overdeveloped sense of empathy and duty. Let's look at how our attachment style influences the degree to which we can empathetically attune to both others and ourselves.

Attachment Styles

Attachment Style Theory is written about extensively in the psychology/ psychotherapy field. The three categories of Attachment Styles are Secure, Avoidant, and Anxious. We can identify where we are on the attachment spectrum by looking at how we experience closeness and connection with others. It's important to understand that each of the three different types connects us with the world in a different way. Each type has a unique way of connecting to others in the outside world.

Many clients I've worked with struggle to feel securely attached within themselves. They therefore live in a world with lots of anxiety and uncertainty and thus are examples of the anxious attachment style. Others I work with feel detached from their emotions; therefore, others perceive them as cold and unfeeling. This particular type of individual often tells me they feel numb inside, and that they are unsure how to reach out to meaningfully connect with others. (These individuals embody the avoidant attachment style.)

This is the avoidant personality. Securely attached individuals have a sensibility that naturally opens and closes in attunement to and connection with people, places, and things in the world. These individuals form healthy attachments (to people, places, and things) and conversely are able to disconnect when needed. (They are obviously examples of the secure attachment style.)

When you reflect back on the time when you were growing up, were your needs met consistently and predictably (healthy attunement)? Did your healthy attunement leave you with a sense that you, as an adult, now understand how to ask for what you need with relative ease? This ability is called secure attachment. It is all about mastering the ability to identify and express your feelings.

Or were your needs met inconsistently and infrequently? If yes is your answer, were you left with an insecure sense that you were needy? Could this be why you are tentative about expressing to others how you feel? This scenario would leave you with an anxious attachment style wherein the world doesn't truly feel safe and welcoming enough for you to be able to express your authentic self.

Or do you recall feeling smothered and overwhelmed by your primary caretakers? Did they intrude upon your privacy, causing you to tone down your verbal expressions? Perhaps you avoided connecting with them, acting as if you didn't need them to meet your needs? Perhaps it wasn't safe to express your needs to them, so you pushed your voice down to self-protect. This pattern leaves you with an avoidant attachment style where you chose to silence your voice for self-protection. As a result, you may minimize your own needs and push others away by creating distance—even when you desire closeness.

Despite the excessive anxiety and avoidance we may have felt living disconnected from our intuitive selves, we can move within the attachment spectrum to transcend these core wounds. There are several ways to do this. Self-talk is a powerful and empathetic reattuning tool to use for attachment style disruption. Reassure yourself by speaking to yourself as if you were a trusted loved one. When reestablishing a baseline of calm to balance out your attachment style, as often as you need to, say things to yourself such as, "You are going to be okay," "I cherish you," "I will treat you with respect and thoughtfulness," "You can express your deepest needs safely," or "You are my treasure."

We draw others in with love, for our attachment system responds to that harmonizing vibration. The establishment and maintenance of a consistently loving relationship starts within us. From there we can expand outward through empowered communication patterns. We are free to plant anything in the garden of our body, our soul, our mind, and our spirit. As with farming, whatever we plant will grow. The soil of earth and of mind sprouts both poisonous plants and edible plants without discrimination. How will you answer Chiron's inward invitation to water, weed, or dig up and replant your inner garden so that you will yield something of meaning and purpose at harvest time?

Our behaviors are used to define who we are. In our modern technological era, people can make up anything about what they are and do and then create a website and social media reality to advertise the false self as if it were fact. Are you representing yourself as who you truly are or are not?

Living in Alignment

I think it's important that we are mindful of the ways we personally conduct ourselves outside of our role as professionals within our given field.

I encourage us to live in congruence. It can be easy to compartmentalize our behaviors in our personal lives and justify them to ourselves.

Have you ever misrepresented who you say you are by living incongruently in your personal life? What do you need to look at and consider changing? What choices do you need to consider or reconsider as you read these words?

Besides the obvious harm that we may cause ourselves by living a life of incongruence, there's the inadvertent harm to others we may cause. I suggest that we regularly check in with ourselves to see how much we are living in concert with who we say we are. Do you truly walk your talk? It's important to know who we are and who we are not.

Chiron encourages us to raise our awareness of self-*regulation* and self-*permissiveness* in order to live harmoniously in our personal and professional lives.

We can empathetically self-attune with honest feedback to ourselves. We can honestly and compassionately assess the areas of our lives that we need to clean up. Once we do that we can look at other aspects of ourselves such as our egos, our weaknesses, our vulnerability, and so on. Or we may need to ask ourselves how to let go of rigidity and allow space for a life that is marked by more spontaneity and joy.

When we become accountable for what we need to shift, we can take responsibility for our words and actions without falling into harsh judgments that can result in self-loathing. Shame and self-criticism can be quite painful. We can be present with the unhealthy parts of our self for longer periods of introspection when we have compassion for those parts of ourselves that may be dysfunctional. For instance, when I began to look at the things in my life that I wanted to change, I learned to work with my guilt and shame. I held space and had empathy for those deeply hurt and wounded parts of me that were responsible for creating behaviors that I then judged myself for. Once I approached my wounding in this fashion, I could extend forgiveness to those parts of myself. This self-forgiveness process changed my life.

I encourage you to lean in to these delicate parts of yourself with compassion and to not hurt yourself with more self-criticism. A thorough exploration of your habits, alongside a gentle excavation of your associated underlying wounds, will help you to transform those aspects of yourself that are so deeply in need of healing.

Meditation as a Healing Modality

If you are healing from addiction, a past trauma, or abuse, or are seeking inner awakening and deeper connection, meditation is a beautiful way to bring yourself into harmony. Meditation is a means of accessing your internal resources. The incorporation of a daily meditation practice is one of the most powerful ways to shift your consciousness from feelings of fear to peace, while also simultaneously releasing stress.

The renowned Tibetan Buddhist and author Pema Chödrön speaks to the benefits of meditation in *When Things Fall Apart*:

Meditation is an invitation to notice when we reach our limit and to not get carried away by hope and fear. Through meditation, we're able to see clearly what's going on with our thoughts and emotions, and we can also let them go. What's encouraging about meditation is that even if we shut down, we can no longer shut down in ignorance. We see very clearly that we're closing off. That in itself begins to illuminate the darkness of ignorance. We're able to see how we run and hide and keep ourselves busy so that we never have to let our hearts be penetrated. And we're also able to see how we could open and relax.

Meditation from a scientific perspective reveals that our brain has the ability to actually remodel itself. Neuroplasticity is our brain's capacity to change and adapt to the environment. The amygdala is the area of our brain that is responsible for emotions, survival instincts, and memory. Neuroplasticity of the amygdala is enhanced because the practice of meditation creates lasting, positive changes to the brain by merging the logical left-brain with the intuitive right-brain hemisphere.

By causing neural pathways in the brain to release the neurotransmitters dopamine and serotonin, meditation calms the central nervous system (CNS) and brings autonomic bodily functions into healthy regulation. These neurotransmitters are responsible for regulating the pleasure and emotional response centers of the brain that relieve anxiety and depression and promote sleep. Meditation also facilitates and improves memory retention, enhances cognitive and functional performance, and increases affective processing.

The personal benefits of meditation can be subtle but increase over time. With practice you might feel a deeper sense of well-being, calm, connection, gratitude, love, possibility, expansion, hope, health, faith, patience, or imagination. These are just a few of the psychological and physical benefits of meditation available to you by just closing your eyes, putting all electronic devices on silent mode, and going within.

Meditation may become a spiritual/religious practice for you as it has become for me. I find that time expands as a result of my practice. I love it and I crave it, and I feel a bit off-center without my daily meditation. Life might not pause for us to meditate; therefore, we must ourselves create that pause each day to see with our inner eyes the vast universe beyond our temporal world.

Through guided and silent meditations that are steeped in spiritual truths based on unconditional love, we can fully connect to a world beyond this one. Some favorite online meditations that I use and recommend are on YouTube. I subscribe to the meditation channel of The Honest Guys. I also enjoy participating in some of the guided meditations offered by Oprah Winfrey and Deepak Chopra through their 21-Day Meditation Experience online, as well as the meditations of

Abraham-Hicks, all of which can be referenced via the resources section of this book.

At other times I sit quietly with my eyes closed and breathe in love, and then exhale love. While driving in traffic or on road trips, to take a break from music, I sing and hum *Om*. I like feeling the vibration of *Om* in my mouth and through my head. I ask that if you take away one thing from this book to put into active practice, beginning a daily meditation practice that centers upon forgiveness and love is probably the best thing you can do for yourself and the planet at this time.

The benefits of meditation can be experienced in as little as four minutes. Start with what you can commit to and expand from there. Over time you will develop the proficiency to drop into your meditative state instantaneously and in any situation. Remember, you are creating an inner sanctum in your mind. A wonderful book to read if you want to learn about ten unique ways to meditate is by my dear friend Benjamin Decker. His book is entitled *Practical Meditation for Beginners: 10 Days to a Happier, Calmer You*. Ben outlines many more ways to meditate other than sitting cross-legged in one spot if that is not your thing!

You can additionally choose to call in ascended masters, spirit guides, animal guides, Reiki healing energy, Jesus, Buddha, the archangels, guardian spirits, and deceased loved ones to be with you during your meditation and to otherwise act in your life as guides. They are always available to be with you. I experience Spirit moving through my spirit body, giving me reassuring thoughts, messages, and course-correcting instructions daily. All of the decisions I make, be they business decisions or personal decisions, are based on the directives I receive in meditation. I ask you to consider increasing your commitment to a meditation practice that you can practice alone, with a partner, or in a group. It's fun to try all of these different settings for meditation in order to see what you favor and energetically gravitate toward.

I realize that not everyone prays. I realize that not everyone believes in a higher spiritual power. Therefore, I ask you to embrace what you *do* believe in. I ask you to embrace what gives you hope, peace, and inspiration, and what sparks desire and purpose within you. I welcome readers of secular belief systems to utilize your own foundational principles for grounding. For some, prayer may be to a god of your own understanding or it may be in the contemplation of a secular thought that carries transformative power. In science, the law of conservation of energy states that energy can neither be created nor destroyed; rather, it transforms from one form to another. Borrowing from this scientific paradigm, allowing your thoughts to transform your current perceived reality may be a healing construct that you embrace from a secular perspective.

Coping with Grief

In working with the psychoastrology of core wounding that Chiron illuminates, it's natural that memories of loss and feelings of sadness, even grief, are exposed. The groundbreaking work of Dr. Elisabeth Kübler-Ross, who identified the different stages of death and dying, is worth mentioning here, as we, too, may find ourselves going through these stages as we excavate painful memories and put them finally to bed. These five stages are denial, anger, bargaining, depression, and acceptance. They were expanded on when she and grief expert David Kessler wrote the classic *On Grief and Grieving,* introducing the stages of grief with transformative pragmatism and compassion.

Kessler, whom I had the pleasure of interviewing on my *All Things Therapy* podcast, has gone beyond the classic five stages to discover a sixth stage: finding meaning. Kessler's newest book is entitled *Finding Meaning: The Sixth Stage of Grief.*

These stages are not steps on a linear timeline, and everyone experiences these stages in an order that is necessary for their own healing.

Often individuals will cycle through these stages multiple times as they are able to assimilate the healing of each stage at deeper and deeper levels of integration. There is no right or wrong way to process and heal from grief and loss; it's a highly individualized and personal process.

The Chakra System

In the service of helping you make friends with your memories (some of which may have been dormant for years), and their accompanying emotions, I offer a comparison utilizing the Hindu chakra system. The chakras are energy systems that begin at the base of our spine and move up and through our body, concluding at the top of the head. Of the 114 chakras in the body, we are most familiar with seven. These seven chakras correlate to various aspects of our lives. The chakra system bridges our material world of body, psychology, and mind with the spiritual world of infinite universal energy.

Often we somaticize our emotions to regions of our body. Indeed, it's well documented that emotions such as sadness, pain, anger, grief, anxiety, depression, and stress manifest in physical regions of our body and may cause disease. By understanding which particular chakra region of our body may be activated by emotional duress, we can aid our healing by treating that chakra with self-care tools, including visualization, sound healing, crystal healing, meditation, energetic bodywork, and Reiki to name just a few.

The Chakra System and the Stages of Grief

The Root Chakra and Denial
The first chakra is found at the very base of the spine. As our *root* chakra, it corresponds to our family of origin, significant occurrences in the past, and our connection to Earth.

The root chakra resonates with the denial stage of grief. For instance, we may struggle to believe that a loved one has died or that our parents were absent or addicted while we were growing up, or that a relationship has ended—and so on. Any major disruption to the root chakra often feels as if our connection to the physical plane, Earth, and everything about earthly life has been severed.

I suggest when we are experiencing this stage of the grief process, we ask for and energetically send love and clarity to our root chakra to aid in its healing. There may be work to do around acceptance and letting go of what we cannot change.

The Sacral Chakra and Anger

The second chakra is found in our groin region and is our sacral chakra, the seat of our sexuality, creativity, and emotion.

I envision the sacral chakra as resonating with the anger stage of grief. Again, we may grapple with unresolved anger toward our caretaker(s) or lover(s) for not meeting our needs, abusing us, abandoning us, dying, or for ways we have abandoned ourselves. In its most positive expression anger can move us to action; it can help us to take proactive steps to establish boundaries. Anger can also be destructive if not regulated. If need be, seek help to address anger management issues. Conversely you may need to give yourself permission to both feel and express your natural anger.

I suggest that when we experience this stage of the grief process, we ask for and energetically send love and peace to our sacral chakra to aid in our healing. Related to any anger that arises, there may be some forgiveness work to do, or some healing work around issues of shame and guilt.

The Solar Plexus Chakra and Bargaining

The third chakra is found in our midsection and is called our solar plexus chakra. This chakra is the seat of our power and confidence.

I envision the solar plexus chakra as resonating with the bargaining stage of grief. Here again, as we struggle to regain our confidence and personal power, we negotiate an endless array of thoughts to mitigate the pain of grief.

As our thoughts circle around past events, we may torture ourselves with "if only" scenarios, such as, if I would have said this or done that, then maybe the outcome would have been different. Or if I had just never relapsed by drinking alcohol again, then maybe she/he would have stayed. Or if only I had directly told so-and-so of my feelings for them, then maybe they would have seen me as a romantic partner. And then we may have, if only I had turned the car left instead of right, they might be alive today. On and on the negotiating goes. After experiencing a loss or having the remembrance of a loss triggered, we can now understand why we struggle so much to reestablish our stability, our grounding, our confidence, and our center.

I suggest that when we experience this stage of the grief process, we ask for and energetically send love and strength to our solar plexus chakra to aid in our healing. There may be themes of regret to process and accept. Associated with this area of the body there may also be judgmental thoughts and self-criticism to reframe, shift, and heal.

The Heart Chakra and Depression

The fourth chakra is the heart chakra, associated with love and compassion. The heart chakra is the mediator and bridge between the lower chakras having to do with sex, aggression, and power and the upper chakras having to do with higher executive functioning and spirituality. This is the region of the body where love emanates from us and is received into us.

I envision the heart chakra as resonating with the depression stage of grief. Over time, as we allow the emotion of sadness to pour out of our hearts through our tears, we allow our emotions and tears to cleanse us of our pain.

I suggest that when we are experiencing this stage of the grief process, we ask for and energetically send love and patience to our heart chakra to aid in our healing. What is associated with the heart region of our body is loss—pure unadulterated loss. The main task is to be patient as we assimilate what comes up during this time. As many rounds of deep emotion come to the surface, remember to be gently loving with yourself and unconditionally patient.

Many of my clients have a hard time allowing themselves to cry when they feel upset. So I went looking for some research that would aid them in giving permission to their bodies to shed a few tears.

It is scientific fact that tears release three stress hormones from the body when we cry. For you science buffs, the hormones are prolactin, adrenocorticotropic hormone (ACTH), and leucine encephalin. These stress hormones *need* to be released for our health and well-being. Dr. William Frey II is credited with this important discovery. I offer this information to you so that you may use it or pass it on to your loved ones or any clients you may have who are overly restrictive in their affect regulation (emotional regulation).

There is a correlation between the degree to which we allow our emotions to flow out from our bodies when we grieve and the amount of energetic room we then create for acceptance, meaning, serenity, peace, and love to enter in.

The Throat Chakra and Acceptance

The fifth chakra is the throat chakra and is associated with truth, communication, and our verbal expression. I envision the throat chakra region of our neck and vocal cords resonating with the acceptance stage of grief.

Here is where our experience of loss begins to come into alignment with our beliefs about life, change, loss, death, and purpose. At this stage we may begin to talk about how a person lived a full life, and we begin to understand the choices they made to get there, even though initially this may have been difficult for us to do. We may begin to talk about how we want to find the lessons in this for us and apply this knowledge by possibly living a more intentional or conscious life, for example. Our focus begins to shift from our grief to ourselves and moving forward. Now we begin to *believe* that *we* will make it through.

I suggest that when you are experiencing this stage of the grief process, you ask for and energetically send love and acknowledgment to your throat chakra to aid in your healing. You will be well served in asking yourself if there is anything you need to say to anyone, since the throat chakra pertains to communication and determining the appropriate format that would facilitate communication best: in person or via a phone call, text, email, or letter. Sometimes when this chakra region is activated it is because we may have some unfinished business to clear up. Encourage yourself to take this step for yourself and for those involved.

The Third Eye Chakra and Finding Meaning

The sixth chakra is known as the third eye. This chakra is located between the eyebrows and is associated with intuition, foresight, and perception. I envision the third eye chakra as resonating with the finding meaning stage of grief. As we become able to weave grief into the fabric of our lives, this chakra represents our ability to transform the earthly (material) pain of the previous stages. Our ability as human beings to create meaning separates us from other species.

When we dive into deep emotions that may be hard to pull ourselves out of, we can use our creativity to develop mantras, hopes, and affirmations to call on in these times of need. Creating new statements that anchor us in our value and worth will also help us move through more emotionally laden moments.

I suggest that when you are experiencing this stage of the grief process, you ask for and energetically send love and focus to your third eye chakra to aid in your healing. The ability to create a narrative about our grief is needed to successfully integrate and find meaning in loss. Unfortunately, some of the hardest losses we face often don't make any sense at all, as in the death of a child or in school shootings. This is where we may turn to spirituality or a higher meaning to cope with such atrocities.

Having a connection to the immaterial or the spiritual, or with nature, literature, art, poetry, music, dance, movies, theater, creativity, and such, are the kinds of things that we can mindfully turn toward and embrace when we feel confused or can't make sense or meaning of a situation involving loss and grief, be they deeply personal or global in scope.

If the latter, you are not alone in struggling to understand some of the atrocities going on in our world today. Many of us have personally experienced some of these violations, including abuse, abandonment, traumatic personal loss, mass shootings, or random acts of violence. Often these things don't make sense to us, and perhaps they never will.

What I *do* know is that points of pain can expand us beyond who we are now and enable us to grow into more beautiful people if we allow this to happen. We do this by tenderly holding on to our precious selves. We also continue our inner work of healing and tap into gratitude for the love that has broken us open to our core and given birth to many small miracles through us.

A good example of this kind of expansion can be seen in the many young people speaking out for gun control in the United States. The student-led March For Our Lives, which occurred on March 24, 2018, is a powerful example of the collective coming together to find healing from grief.

In so many ways, this book is my personal response to being broken open to my core, and in my inability to understand, I began to write. In this creative form I have found peace and meaning.

The Crown Chakra and Life after Death/Afterlife

The seventh chakra, the crown chakra, is located at the top of the head. This is the chakra that gives us access to higher states of consciousness and knowing. It connects us to universal knowledge, the infinite and the immaterial, all of which are beyond our conscious reckoning given our current time/space reality on Earth.

If another stage of grief were to be offered, I speculate that it might be a stage related to life after death or the afterlife. Many people have religious, personal, or spiritual beliefs on the matter; others aren't sure what happens after we die. We all think about it and speculate. This stage could contribute to answering the question we have asked for thousands of years and may ask forever: What lies beyond our physical death?

5

Finding Chiron in Your Chart

And Understanding the Astrological Houses

In chapters 6–17 we will journey through the meaning of Chiron in each of the twelve signs of the zodiac. Remember that reading this book in its entirety will equip you to navigate, cope with, and heal issues we all face as human beings. I found that although Chiron's sign and house placement in my natal chart indicates one major area of core wounding, I have had issues in my life that relate to *all* of the other placements of Chiron.

You will find a thorough look at Chiron valuable as well, given that so many of us have experienced loss, abandonment, or a breakup; felt disconnected, overwhelmed, undervalued, neglected, or blocked from creatively; been addicted, had a major health issue, or felt the need to create community. That said, however, you will want to pay *special* attention to your core wound as indicated by your birth chart.

Finding Chiron in Your Birth Chart

The table on the following page lists the sign location of Chiron by year and the core wounding associated with that sign so that you may

FINDING YOUR CHIRON AND CORE WOUNDING BY DATE OF BIRTH

Astrological Sign	Birth Dates	Cause or Source of Core Wounding "in" or "because of"
Chiron in Aries	April 1968–June 1976 and May 2018–June 2026	Value and worth
Chiron in Taurus	April 1927–May 1933 and June 1976–June 1983	Neglect
Chiron in Gemini	June 1933–August 1937 and June 1983–June 1988	Empathetic attunement
Chiron in Cancer	September 1937–June 1941 and June 1988–July 1991	Abandonment
Chiron in Leo	June 1941–August 1943 and July 1991–September 1993	Creativity
Chiron in Virgo	August 1943–October 1944 and September 1993–September 1995	Management of physical health and routines
Chiron in Libra	December 1944–November 1946 and September 1995–December 1996	Personal independence
Chiron in Scorpio	December 1946–December 1948 and January 1997–September 1999	Experience and expression of power
Chiron in Sagittarius	December 1948–November 1951 and September 1999–December 2001	Truth and illusion
Chiron in Capricorn	November 1951–January 1955 and December 2001–February 2005	Responsibility, achievement, and success
Chiron in Aquarius	February 1955–March 1960 and March 2005–February 2011	Connection and community
Chiron in Pisces	March 1960–March 1968 and March 2011–April 2018	Self-care and the immaterial world

quickly find the astrological sign Chiron was in at your birth and identify your deepest area of core wounding.

Your Chiron sign identifies *what* your core wounding is, and your
Chiron house placement identifies *how* this wound manifests in
your life. To locate Chiron's house placement in your astrological
natal chart go to www.nolatherapy.com/chiron and click on "My
Chiron." A new page will pop up with a box in which to enter your
birth data. You will need to enter the date, place, and time of your
birth as accurately as you can. If you don't have exact times or dates,
give your best educated guess, and go with the results. After submit-
ting and confirming your data, you will be given your ascendant, sign,
and natal chart. In the natal chart Chiron will be marked by the ⚷
symbol. Notice how the symbol for Chiron looks like a key; this key
symbolizes the unlocking of the unconscious, or consciousness shifting. Hover your cursor over the Chiron symbol, and the astrological
sign and house of Chiron in your birth chart will be noted in the
shaded box just above the chart.

How to Apply This Information

In the following chapters you will learn about Chiron's twelve areas of
core wounding illuminated in each of the twelve signs of the zodiac.
This information will bring greater understanding and clarity to patterns and circumstances in your life as well as help you to initiate
changes that lead to growth, healing, and fulfillment. At the beginning of each of the subsequent chapters, there is a box that expresses
more specifically how someone with a wounded or healed Chiron in
this placement might feel. At the end of each chapter, affirmations and
takeaways are offered for use in grounding yourself in a new paradigm
of thinking.

Each affirmation and takeaway point has been meditated on and
infused with Reiki healing energy to assist in your healing journey.

Using Affirmations

Each affirmation is tailor made for the specific core wound that it seeks to heal. The affirmations are intended for your use in replacing the underlying beliefs caused by Chiron's specific core wounding.

Again, affirmations are generally most effective when written down and placed in various areas of your home, office, car, purse, or wallet, to be read silently or aloud throughout the day.

Stating them out loud is a stronger way of declaring who you are becoming. Over time, repeating these words to yourself will become the foundation of your new beliefs as they take root in your mind, influence your emotions, and then inform your decisions and actions.

Allow yourself to breathe in each affirmation and smile as you read it. State these affirmations out loud whenever possible as a declaration of who you are becoming. Commit yourself to allowing the affirmations to create internal shifts of awareness in your psyche.

Frequent exposure to each affirmation increases its power to transform your thought patterns, thus positively affecting your underlying belief systems. These changes in beliefs generated from within your mind reframe the narrative of your experiences. Over time those inner shifts in perception inspire you to engage with people, places, and things differently. You will be showing up differently in your life, and life will show you that evidence by the wonderful new manifestations you begin to create

As time goes by and as you begin to feel happier, you will naturally be encouraged to create beautiful new experiences. You will be changing your life from the inside out.

Once the affirmations in this book and others like it have been implanted in your psyche, go ahead and create your own affirmations to use and meditate on. Have fun, and be creative with this process. Because you are so familiar with your deepest needs, you know best the shadowy recesses of your mind that need to be exposed to the light of forgiveness and love. You will find that your affirmations support the healing that is needed for you to be able to step into a greater version of yourself. When you take individual responsibility for your own healing, the cumulative effect of your work is emotionally, physically, and energetically beneficial to all.

The Takeaways

These takeaways of text that I've added to the narrative give you examples of practical steps that you can use today to change your life. By trying them out one at a time, you can experiment with expanding or regulating boundaries to create closeness or distance, pausing to check in with yourself before you overcommit, evaluating specific areas of your life for adjustment and optimization, speaking your truth to a loved one whom you have feared disappointing, or taking the step of entering therapy for the first time. Each takeaway is tailored for the specific core wounding it addresses.

Understanding Your House Placement

Each of the astrological houses corresponds to a certain area, aspect, realm, or time of your life, as outlined in the list below.

First House: Your body, personality, and the traits you possess that are most noticeable and apparent to the outside world. This includes such things as temperament, leadership style, the ego, and the way you take initiative (or don't take initiative).

Second House: Your values and possessions, including your personal values and priorities, morals, personal finances, and material wealth.

Third House: Communication and its lessons, communication devices and technology, siblings or lack of siblings, and grade school years.

Fourth House: Sense of place, security, nurturing, emotional conditioning, the emotional climate of your childhood, your family of origin (both the people you grew up with and the home itself), your current family composition, and your current physical home.

Fifth House: Creativity, children, play, self-expression, romance, and pleasure.

Sixth House: Professional work, daily routines, service work, exercise, fitness, diet, physical health, and disease.

Seventh House: Contracts and partnerships pertaining to business relationships and personal relationships, including marriage and divorce.

Eighth House: Intensely shared emotional experiences, including birth, death, sex, transformation, other people's money and property, mystical experiences, spirituality, and metaphysics.

Ninth House: Politics, religion, the law, news, foreign travel, areas of study, higher education, one's philosophy of life and world view.

Tenth House: Your public reputation, social status, image, persona, issues of fame, honor, achievement and recognition, career.

Eleventh House: Groups, associations, friends, social justice, and humanitarian causes.

Twelfth House: The unconscious mind, the shadow, addictions, the outer realms of society (jails, psychiatric hospitals, outliers), endings and completions, spirituality, and the use of one's imagination in the arts, film, dance, music, and poetry.

Included in the more in-depth descriptions of the houses below are questions to consider about your own relationship with the houses. Again, it is important to note the areas and aspects that each house represents, but give extra attention to the house where Chiron is located in your personal birth chart.

As noted, your house specifically indicates where your core wounding manifests in your life. To guide your healing efforts, view "Questions to consider," which are found under the house that your

Chiron is found in. By blending the information that your Chiron sign and house placement provide, you discover a deeper understanding of how the psychoastrology of Chiron operates behind the scenes, and in this you become empowered to make the unconscious conscious to better direct your life.

For example, if your Chiron lies in Gemini in the twelfth house, perhaps your core wound in empathic attunement has manifested as the misunderstood child becoming the addicted teen (a tendency of the twelfth house). And perhaps healing comes in the form of expressing your authentic thoughts through an imaginative twelfth house medium such as art, dance, or spirituality.

The Astrological Houses

An astrological chart visually looks like a round clock, starting with the first house located between eight and nine o'clock and continuing all the way around, counterclockwise, ending with the twelfth house, which is between nine and ten o'clock. Under each house description is text pertaining to the various aspects and areas of your life to pay attention to. These are the regions of your life to look at, question yourself about, and create change in. The house placement of Chiron illuminates the areas of your life, aspects of your personality, and behavioral patterns that contain blind spots and challenges, and therefore growth opportunities for you.

The house descriptions are as follows:

First House
Again, the first house has to do with the personality traits of yours that are most noticeable and apparent to the outside world. These are traits such as temperament, leadership style, your consciousness, ego, the body, and the way you take initiative.

Questions to consider are:

❧ How have you censored or limited your expression of self, identity, or personality? Work with the guided meditations and affirmations suggested throughout this book to increase self-esteem and self-confidence where needed.

❧ Are you able to set limits with yourself and others when needed? How can you set clear boundaries having to do with where you will and will not invest your energy and efforts?

Give yourself a buffer of time to make decisions, and permit yourself to answer with yes, no, or maybe. Give yourself permission to be authentic. Allow your true self to shine.

Second House

The second house has to do with your values and possessions. This pertains specifically to your value system, morals, personal finances, and material wealth.

Questions to consider are:

❧ What are the ways you've had struggles or problems with in the areas of the second house?

❧ Does money seem to be an all-or-nothing type of situation for you? If so, then you might want to consider developing a secure attachment style to money versus an anxious or avoidant attachment style to money, which may help you be able to draw in and maintain the material resources you need.

❧ How can you spend within your means while looking for ways to increase or diversify your income? How can you bring your spending habits into congruence with your financial earnings?

A skilled practitioner can help you with the emotional/energetic component of your relationship to money. Meeting with a financial planner may be helpful in restructuring your finances and future planning.

A way to increase the flow of material resources toward you is to identify charities to donate to or volunteer service opportunities. Clarify what your value system is and what it is not.

Bring yourself into alignment by determining a unique and personal moral code that reflects your values.

Make amends with people where needed. Identify guidelines or adopt a spiritual path that informs and guides your behavior. A place to start might be to live by the golden rule, meaning that you treat people in the manner that you yourself would like to be treated.

In order to consistently prosper, do your best to live from a place of love and kindness in all matters that pertain to your heart and your finances.

Third House

The third house in general has to do with communication and its lessons, communication devices, siblings/lack of siblings, and grade school years.

Identify ways that you may have intentionally or unintentionally communicated inaccurate information. Seek to bring your spoken and written word into harmony with what you wish to convey and how you wish to be heard and perceived.

Questions to consider are:

- ⚷ Are there unresolved issues with your siblings that you might consider resolving? For instance, maybe you wanted your parents to have another child so that you wouldn't be an only child. Speaking to your parent(s)/caretakers may be an option so that you can have resolution in this area if you think they would be open to hearing your concerns.

- ⚷ Do your issues from grade school need to be revisited and healed with the help of a healing practitioner or by talking to a trusted loved one?

⚹ Were you bullied in school, or did you bully others?

I definitely recommend a healing professional to help navigate the effects of bullying, but in any event it's important to your well-being to take some time to be with your younger inner self as you answer these questions.

Fourth House

The fourth house has to do with your sense of place, home, security, nurturing, and emotional conditioning. This house involves your family of origin (both the people in the family whom you grew up with and the home itself), and your adult family/home.

Questions to consider are:

⚹ Was there consistent love and nurturing in your home?

⚹ Was there violence or unpredictability, or did your family move frequently?

⚹ What was the emotional climate in your family of origin?

Creating order, safety, beauty, peace, and joy to any degree is important to your healing. A place to start is by clearing out clutter. Donate or sell articles of clothing you haven't worn in the past two years and, especially, purge items that bring up negative feelings about past experiences or relationships.

Making these shifts and changes in your living environment will have a positive effect on your emotional well-being and recalibrate your experience of and relationship with what "home" can be for you today.

Look for ways to make your residence feel like a true home. Healing comes from making your living environment a haven of love, peace, and tranquility.

Fifth House

The fifth house pertains to creativity, children, play, self-expression, romance, and pleasure. Identify ways to tap into and express your creativity. Let your inner child be expressive. Questions to consider are:

- How do you find and experience pleasure?
- What makes you laugh?
- What do you enjoy? Is it nature, sports, theater, art, cooking, music, intimacy, sexuality, romance, adventure, time with your children, volunteering, traveling, or a combination of the above?

Transforming or removing blocks in your belief system that have to do with your ability to create, play, experience pleasure, and romance will free you up to new experiences.

You may consider talking to friends and asking how they address these topics and what *they* do. You may engage the help of a healing practitioner or you may want to take time out to journal about your dreams and desired manifestations. Or you may engage in a healing meditation practice.

Allow yourself to explore your desires and engage with as many of them as you can in order to enhance this area of your life.

Sixth House

In general, the sixth house has to do with your professional work, daily routines, service work, and physical health.

Specific areas pertaining to your health include fitness, diet, exercise, and any proclivity to disease. Are you experiencing health problems, or do you have recurring health problems?

Questions to consider are:

- ❧ How might you strengthen your immune system to help prevent illness, disease, and discomfort?
- ❧ Are you taking your medications as prescribed?
- ❧ Are you attending your yearly wellness physicals with your doctor and following his or her recommendations?
- ❧ Do you have a colonoscopy at the required intervals?
- ❧ If you are a woman, do you see your gynecologist for an annual visit, to have a Pap smear and arrange for a mammogram? If you're a man, do you have your prostate checked at the required intervals?
- ❧ Do you eat a healthy diet and exercise regularly each week?
- ❧ Is your weight within an optimal range for your height? If not, you might want to research and adopt a dietary program to adhere to. Perhaps meet with a nurse, doctor, nutritionist, naturopath, or similar type of health care practitioner for consultation and guidance.
- ❧ Do you have a daily routine that reflects a healthy work/life balance?
- ❧ Do you have an outlet to fulfill your desire to be of service by being plugged into volunteer or service work?

These are all areas to consider and examine to see what adjustments you may need to make in order to be functioning at optimal levels.

Seventh House

The seventh house has to do with partnerships and contracts, both personal and professional, including marriage, divorce, and business.

Questions to consider are:

- ❧ Are you making the money you deserve to earn, or do you need to negotiate pay that is congruent with your expertise and years of experience?

꘏ Does a current contract need to be renegotiated or terminated if it no longer serves you?

꘏ Is your intimate relationship or marriage offtrack; does it need some attention?

꘏ Do you and your partner both feel loved, fulfilled, supported, seen, heard, and satisfied?

꘏ If you are single, are you becoming a person whom you would want to be with?

꘏ Are there things in your life that you need to forgive yourself for in order to be emotionally free to pursue and create the relationship you want to have?

Look to these areas of your life for insight and make appropriate changes where necessary.

Eighth House

The eighth house has to do with intense, emotional, shared experiences such as birth, death, sex, transformation, and other people's property/finances. This house also is associated with mystical experiences, spirituality, and metaphysics.

Questions to consider are:

꘏ How do you maintain your psychological and spiritual health/connection?

꘏ What do you need to examine and possibly let go of in your personal life?

꘏ In a broader sense, is it time to let go of other people, places, or things who no longer serve you and develop new connections in these areas?

꘏ Do you have spiritual practices in place that resonate with your soul's need to connect deeply to Source, or are you going through the motions to comply in some way that doesn't serve your deepest longings?

❧ Do you have connections with others that satisfy your need to explore yourself and others through intense, shared experiences?

❧ Are you living fully plugged into what fires up your passion physically, emotionally, psychologically, sexually, and spiritually?

❧ Do you handle other people's finances responsibly?

If not, make the necessary changes in order to live fully energized in each of these areas.

Ninth House

The ninth house pertains to issues of politics, religion, news, foreign travel, and higher education and includes our life philosophy and worldview.

Questions to consider are:

❧ Are there classes you may be interested in taking or a program of study you have put aside to fulfill other responsibilities? This could be a time to revisit those dreams and goals and formulate a plan to achieve them now.

❧ Do you have any outstanding legal issues to address and resolve?

❧ Do you want to take up a cause and work to bring justice to a disenfranchised population?

❧ Are there travel destinations you've dreamed of visiting?

❧ Can you begin to research that dream trip to take in the future by planning where you would like to stay, the sights you would like to see, the food and drink you imagine yourself enjoying?

Allow for exploration of these areas, and plug into them in any capacity possible in order to live into your full potential.

Tenth House

The tenth house has to do with your public reputation, social status, fame, honor, achievement, and career.

Questions to consider are:

§ Are you projecting the desired image of yourself on social media, at your workplace, in your family, with your friends, and in all of your relationships?

§ Are you living beyond your means so that you appear to be of a certain social status, and feeling stress as a result?

§ Are you being recognized for your work and accomplishments?

§ Are you giving credit to the correct individual(s) so they, too, can be acknowledged?

§ Are you living congruently within your value system?

§ Do you work just to bring in money or are you impassioned about your vocation or avocation?

Since this house has to do with the public persona and recognition of that persona, clear up any misunderstandings or mishaps in order to project the best and most appropriate image of yourself so that you are accurately perceived and acknowledged.

Eleventh House

The eleventh house has to do with groups, associations, friends, social justice, and humanitarian causes. It's important for your happiness that you stay connected to others. Be sure to reach out to others when you begin to feel lonely or isolated.

Questions to consider are:

§ Do you have meaningful associates and friendships, and do you allot time to nurturing these relationships?

§ Do you have enough involvement with organizations and

community events that speak to your heart and mind?

- ⚬ Are you involved as a volunteer for an organization, or might you create an event to help with a cause dear to you?
- ⚬ Is there a social justice issue for which you'd like to start a petition or a crowdfunding campaign? Perhaps you might attend a public protest/rally? Let your voice be heard because it counts!

Twelfth House

The twelfth house pertains to the unconscious mind, the shadow side, addictions, and the outer realms of society such as jails and psychiatric hospitals. This house also has to do with endings and completions, spirituality, and the use of one's imagination in the arts, film, dance, music, and poetry.

Questions to consider are:

- ⚬ Are there hidden areas of your life needing to be brought into your consciousness?
- ⚬ Can you employ healing modalities from the arts, film, dance, music, theater, movies, or poetry, for instance, which might replace an addiction or a compulsion?
- ⚬ Do you need to resolve a legal matter?
- ⚬ Are you judging yourself from a past offense and, in so doing, need to begin the process of finding forgiveness for yourself?
- ⚬ Do you keep a dream journal?
- ⚬ How do you utilize your intuition in conducting your personal and professional affairs?

In the twelfth house lives a deeply spiritual assignment of Chiron's core wounding that is healed through connection to the immaterial/spiritual and through the development of self-care practices.

If this is where Chiron is located in your chart, you are in a powerful placement to be able to transcend an addiction/compulsion to drugs, alcohol, sex, exercise, or food. Equally so, you are able to resolve any legal issue, physical health issue or mental health issue through spirituality, nature, and service. Look within yourself in an honest way, and ask to see what you truly need to address. You can improve your connection to the wounded, unloved parts of yourself by facing your illusions and transcending them with authenticity.

6

Chiron in Aries

....

Core Wounding in Value and Worth

Wounded Chiron Feels

No right to exist

Fundamentally "wrong"

Overly self-sufficient

Healed Chiron Feels

Lovable

Worthy

A right to exist

Chiron entered the sign of Aries on April 17, 2018, and will spend about eight years here. Historically, when Chiron occupied the sign of Aries, changes in laws were initiated pertaining to human rights, personal freedoms, and social change. Chiron in Aries is about taking action to break free. Chiron in Aries brought sexual revolution during the Roaring Twenties and during the time of Prohibition. (Well, we all know that Prohibition really meant no inhibition!) Homosexuality was decriminalized in East Germany in 1968 and West Germany in 1969, with Mexico, Guatemala, Japan, and some states in the United States following suit. The groundbreaking Stonewall riots occurred in 1969 in Manhattan, and the first LGBT Pride Parade occurred in New York City in 1970. In 1972 the Watergate scandal broke, and in 1974 our president resigned from office. All of these events, and even more seminal ones, occurred internationally under the powerful influence of Chiron in Aries, which encourages us to take action, to speak our voice, to stand up for our rights, and to be authentically who *we* are! How does Chiron in Aries affect you as an individual?

With Chiron in Aries, your relentless search for a stable and strong identity drives your life experience. At the same time, the psychoastrology of Chiron in Aries creates a concurrent and conflicting emotional experience wherein you may feel as if you already have an identity, but you invariably judge it to be weak. As a result, time and time again you find yourself in situations where you minimize your own needs. In the worst-case scenarios, your needs have been neglected by others. This episodic lack of attunement to your needs speaks to your self-diminishment and unresolved sense of value and worth.

Because you have become so attuned to others and their needs, sometimes it may be hard for you to even know what you want. It may seem that you have lost connection to yourself. It's as if your selfhood may have been eclipsed and you are invariably not seen, heard, or validated.

This experience is disempowering to your self-confidence, and your ability to attract what you truly desire is obstructed. Instead of directly expressing your own needs and to protect yourself from the pain of being undervalued and treated dismissively, you employ coping mechanisms of compensation and adaptation.

You run the risk of burnout in your profession and being unhappy in your personal life. This occurs because of consistent people pleasing and putting the needs of others first. Overextending yourself is an ingrained habit you employ to keep conflict low. You feel that working to keep the peace in your family, group, or organization is a must.

You feel exhausted and depleted as a result. You may suffer privately from feelings of isolation while simultaneously hoping that one day you will suddenly be seen, loved, and valued for the generous person that you really are.

The way you approach love has been built around a false belief that you have to work hard to be loved. Let me invite you to consider something you did not learn in your childhood, but that you can now step into and fully embrace. Here it is: You *don't* have to work hard to be loved, you *are* lovable, you *are* worthy, and you *are* good enough—just as you are.

Your work is to let go of the self-deprecating and defeating beliefs that hurt you. While allowing others to manage conflicts on their own, you can learn to possess and then express your personal preferences directly in positive and meaningful ways.

The psychological overlay of a wounded sense of self, coupled with the undervaluing of self, leads to feelings of depression, isolation, and unworthiness, resulting in a sense of confusion about the path forward.

While you are experiencing these difficult emotions, it's easy to turn to maladaptive coping behaviors such as harming oneself through substance abuse/dependence, or holding onto relationships and associations that no longer feel good, or serve your highest good.

Often self-criticism and judgment of ourselves keep us stuck in an unhealthy relationship or situation. We don't want to give up and move on, so we may stay and self-medicate instead. Here is how Pema Chödrön describes this pattern:

> Most of us do not take these situations as teachings. We automatically hate them. We run like crazy. We use all kinds of ways to

escape—all addictions stem from this moment when we meet our edge and we just can't stand it. We feel we have to soften it, pad it with something, and we become addicted to whatever it is that seems to ease the pain. Instead, when we meet our edge, we can realize that we have a profound growth opportunity before us. To just be with the experience, allowing the quality of what we're feeling to pierce us to the heart, without reacting or repressing.

Self-harming behaviors reinforce our sense of unimportance because, after the fact, we stand in condemnatory judgment of ourselves. We may present a public image of having it all together, yet we may suffer privately. Lessening the grip of self-judgment and increasing the presence of self-love in our lives creates the psychic and energetic space to cultivate our value and worth. By committing to the prioritization of our needs, we learn to value ourselves. Coupled with pulling back from our overextended state, we shift and begin to embody our true value.

We must gently and lovingly hold ourselves accountable for not having shown up for ourselves in the past. However, we are not unworthy for having made mistakes. Our identity is not engraved with our mistakes. Every misstep is an opportunity to learn and grow, and then do something different the next time.

If prayer is a part of your life and a tool that you use, I offer this prayer by Marianne Williamson from her book *A Year of Miracles*. It may help you view yourself through eyes of compassion:

I have made mistakes for which I atone, but my mistakes are not who I am. Today may I be who I am called to be, that my thoughts and actions might glorify love.

Within my heart, as within all hearts, there is the light of a divine creator. Nothing I have done, or that others have done; nothing I have thought, or that others have thought, can dim the light that dwells in me. I pray to see the perfection in others, that I might see it in myself. I pray for the strength to forgive all others, that I might forgive myself. I pray for the power to love all others, that I might love myself.

Because the wounding to our core value and sense of worth occurred in childhood, our inner child needs to be given messages of empathy and tenderness. Our inner child is a younger ego construct within our adult ego state. She/he/they typically makes her/himself/themselves known when we feel hurt, vulnerable, anxious, avoidant, jealous, upset, ungrounded, angry, fearful, or self-doubting. Our adult ego state often tells that vulnerable inner child self to go away, be quiet, or hide. If you repress these uncomfortable feelings of vulnerability to the point where the feelings become unconscious, they may begin to drive your life in the direction of self-sabotage.

Transformation and healing of this wound comes through sending your inner child, adolescent, and adult ego states nurturing and love with messages of support and empathy. Because the wounding to our core value and sense of worth occurred in childhood, our inner child needs to be given messages of empathy and tenderness. Transformation and healing of this wound comes by sending your inner child nurturing and love with messages of support and empathy.

This begins a process of insourcing healthy self-esteem and positive feelings for yourself, instead of outsourcing that job to others, which can result in a roller coaster of emotions for you.

Daily guided meditations that focus on forgiveness and love can accelerate the healing process. A plan of regular self-care can include setting aside time and space to think and assess whether or not your commitments are truly serving you. Or are "responsibilities" just an easier way for you to stay busy, thereby keeping unpleasant emotions at bay?

That which is avoided eventually bubbles up to the surface, often unexpectedly. Addressing underlying feelings of anger, shame, and regret from past experiences of abuse, or instances where you gave your power away, will clear out elements of your shadow that sit unacknowledged, only to burst forth when triggered by a current event or situation. Those unattended feelings then create a negative feedback loop wherein your legitimate needs cannot be met.

Below is a journal entry of mine from 2001, which I discovered recently when I was compiling resources to write this book. It exemplifies my inner struggle with feelings of shame, anger, and regret, which I was working through at that time. Those feelings flourished because I was not seen, heard, or valued as a young person growing up.

At the end of the journal entry I realized that instead of seeking approval from others, I must validate myself. This realization allowed me to begin healing my core wounds. In so doing, I enabled myself to access my inner knowing and began to step into my personal power. Here is my journal entry. See if it resonates with you.

My heart locks herself away, safe from the pain, safe from the rejection, safe from the criticism, safe from the fear, safe from your abandonment. The walls of fear keep her protected from your hurt.

In a distant land long ago, the voice of her ancients spoke out to her; their voices were loud. They said, "We don't see you, we don't need you, we don't even love you, be gone from our land!" So away she went. For years she has been running, thinking all is well with her soul.

But she can never get far from the voice of her ancients. They speak through others she has trusted enough to love. They betray her through their actions.

What is invisible to their feeble eyes does exist. Locked in the solitude of her heart, she feels their failure—their failure to see her.

The walls of fear that promise to protect her from pain paralyze her from speaking the truth of love.

How can my own heart keep me from revealing what I need? The walls are useless, but they are strong.

One day she plans to do things differently. I believe that day is here—and so suddenly. She wonders whether her ancients from the distant land will notice her? Whether they do or not—I will.

As a Chiron in Aries individual you have a deep need to be seen and heard in relation to your power, ability, and creativity. Let me reiterate that: From deep within yourself, you can validate your power, lovability, and creativity. Others will then simply begin to mirror back what you have learned to hold true for yourself. Forgiving yourself allows for a wellspring of creative energy to flow through you purely, joyously, and without obstruction. In matters most important, you have at your fingertips a seemingly endless supply of energy that can generate great change in yourself and in the world.

One of the many individuals whose work has helped me reach beyond my own limiting beliefs is Rapid Transformational Therapist (RTT) Marisa Peer. She is an internationally known therapist, speaker, and author. Peer has created an amazing YouTube video filmed at Mindvalley Academy entitled, "I Am Enough." If you have not watched this video and are an individual with Chiron's core wounding in Aries, I am instructing you to *run,* not walk, to your phone or computer, pull it up immediately, and listen. Marisa hits at the core of our wounding by pointing out that we truly are enough, exactly as we are, in this and every moment.

For us to create lasting changes in our mind it is necessary to regularly expose ourselves to the thought patterns we want to create. This process of change serves to continually disrupt negative, maladaptive thought patterns. Positive support systems serve as constant reminders that our true value is grounded in the simple preciousness of our worth. Over time this practice starts to rapidly shift the negative core beliefs we have held on to about ourselves.

The shadow side of Chiron in Aries may be buried in your unconscious and manifest in behaviors that incur the unwanted criticism of others, instead of bringing about the understanding and empathy you wish to receive. This would manifest as a tendency toward martyrdom for the Chiron in Aries individual. Martyrdom is an utter depletion of yourself wherein you believe that you are sacrificing yourself to help others, but you are criticized. Despite your best efforts, you are perceived negatively because your help is often unsolicited and unwanted.

When you find yourself in this place, it can be helpful to ask yourself where you violated your own inner knowing and boundaries, or where you believed that you knew better than someone else and therefore thought you were helping them by sharing your unsolicited advice. These unhealthy patterns can leave you feeling overextended, resulting in an extreme sense of mental and emotional exhaustion.

So take responsibility for positioning yourself as martyr. Anticipate situations where you think you may find yourself feeling less than or in a state of disempowerment. There is no need to be the martyr anymore, or to give unsolicited advice even if you believe you actually *do* know better. You can instead ask others if they're interested in hearing your suggestions.

Become comfortable with your new life path, and with allowing others to find their own way. "I can't work harder than my client is willing to," is a saying commonly uttered by therapists of all stripes. Set internal limits to curb yourself in this self-defeating pattern of doing too much for others. You can learn ways of letting others know that you support them without taking on their guilt, fear, stress, or shame, or by trying to figure things out for them. They must do that work on their own, in their own way, and in their own perfect time.

ॐ *Takeaways*

- Before replying to someone who makes a request of your time, energy, or resources, which you may feel uncertain about complying with, take a few moments (or up to several days if necessary) to take a personal inventory. This will give you time to determine if a commitment will enhance or detract from your maintenance of harmony and balance. If someone has asked you to do something for them, you may consider replying to them with a statement such as: "Maybe. Let me check my schedule and get back to you on that." Use this statement until you are able to set healthy limits in the moment. This allows you a buffer of time to quiet yourself and check in as to how you *really* feel. The goal you are working toward is to be available to others while maintaining your personal energy reserves.

- Set healthy internal limits as you are acquainting yourself with the downtime necessary for your own self-care and to meet your existing responsibilities. The goal is to break the cycle of spreading yourself too thin. If a commitment no longer suits you, learn that it's okay to renegotiate that commitment. People will respect your directness and integrity. And as a result of respecting yourself, you will feel genuinely good about yourself.

- Be aware of any underlying thoughts and beliefs that may cause upsetting feelings, which can lead to actions of maladaptive coping and ultimately self-sabotage. Speak to yourself as if you were giving praise to another individual who is doing a great job! Give yourself the same positive messages of encouragement each and every day.

❧ Be your own inner coach and cheerleader. Examples of encouraging messages to tell yourself are: "I am doing a great job," "I am making progress," "I love you so much," "I am so valuable," "I am growing," "Let's keep going," and "You are doing great."

❧ *Affirmations*

"I own my right to exist."
"Value lies within."
"I am enough."
"I am worthy."

7

Chiron in Taurus

Core Wounding by Neglect

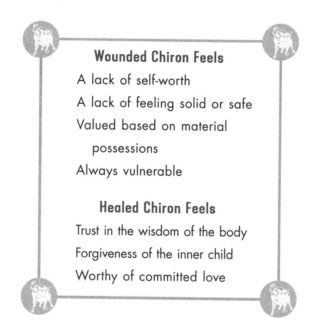

Wounded Chiron Feels

A lack of self-worth

A lack of feeling solid or safe

Valued based on material
possessions

Always vulnerable

Healed Chiron Feels

Trust in the wisdom of the body

Forgiveness of the inner child

Worthy of committed love

The sign of Taurus regulates our material resources and our value system. The psychoastrology of Chiron in Taurus creates a sense of lack in those two areas, ranging from neglect to being completely without. Themes of ethics, morality, and finances are highlighted in this placement of Chiron.

Chiron was in Taurus during Black Tuesday—when the New York Stock Exchange completely collapsed on October 29, 1929—and the ensuing Great Depression began. Al Capone's prison sentence for tax evasion in 1931 and the opening of the FBI Crime Lab in 1932 are two examples of the healing of our country's value system that took place under Chiron in Taurus, demonstrating this placement's ability to heal and support finances and moral values. The next Chiron in Taurus generation born in the early 1980s became known as the millennials. They came of age during the Great Recession of the late 2000s and early 2010s. The recession featured historically high levels of unemployment among young people, causing long-term economic and social challenges to this generation. Themes of ethics, morality, and finances are highlighted by this placement of Chiron in Taurus. What does this mean for *you* as an individual with Chiron in Taurus?

Here is a picture for you if your Chiron is in the sign of Taurus: In your upbringing there may have been instances and experiences of neglect that resulted in a damaged sense of your self-worth and self-esteem. You may have been sexually coerced, thus making you a survivor of sexual abuse, trauma, assault, rape, exploitation, or human trafficking.

In your desire to heal you may have unconsciously employed defense mechanisms to repress feelings of shame, vulnerability, and powerlessness. By using compensatory methods to feel valuable and in control and to conceal low self-esteem, you may have made great efforts to pursue financial gain, material wealth/possessions, or sexual conquests in order to assert a sense of personal power and control over your life.

It can be challenging for you to feel vulnerable because you may label that feeling as weakness. In the past, it often wasn't safe for you to be vulnerable. Vulnerability left you powerless and at the whim of those with ill intentions, who eventually hurt you.

As a result, fantasies of power and dominance may pervade your imagination because of the experience of having no power as a victim.

Taking the victimized child's power back in healthy ways is at the core of your healing. These drives may cause you to compromise ethics that conflict with your true value system. As a result, your desire for mastery and your attempts to heal remain elusive.

An important step in your healing that must not be bypassed is to feel the initial wound of neglect that was born at the core of your victimization and powerlessness. It was not your fault. You were innocent. You don't need to wall off from your consciousness the memories and accompanying feelings that may be buried deep within you, or contained within alternate personality constructs. You can learn to find love for yourself and peace of mind. Initially you may do this in the context of a safe and secure healing relationship. You can also find nurturance with people who understand what you have been through and want to be a safe haven for you. You can learn to feel truly safe in your own skin and in your own body without engaging in peak experience activities, behaviors, or purchases that generate extreme highs of pleasure that soothe you only temporarily and then let you down and leave you feeling depressed and powerless.

Repairing and recalibrating your sense of value in regard to your finances, body image, sexuality, and material possessions is necessary. Misguided attempts to repair your self-worth and esteem by maintaining a falsely projected body image or reputation can actually create new financial, emotional, physical, psychological, and spiritual traumas.

As a way to source power from your projected identity, work (for example) may provide you with temporary external validation, while instead you could draw upon internal validation that's sourced in meaning and purpose by being of service or by helping others. Conversely, because of your childhood background and experiences, you may have powerful intuitive abilities. You have the potential to be creative with healing modalities that flow from a place of your inner radiance, strength, and resilience.

I encourage you to tune in to the inner knowing of your higher self.

Chiron's message to you is that you do not have to continue to hide and defend against the orbital pull of your personal experiences of neglect, which you have felt periodically throughout your life. This neglect has resulted in appropriate feelings of grief, sadness, vulnerability, and help-lessness. It is now time to face the deep interior work that's required to heal the psychoastrology of Chiron's core wounding.

By facing your inner wounding and choosing to step into your fear or denial, you will open up to:

- Learning to love yourself and your body fully in ways that are not performance based or appearance driven
- Being able to love others just as they are
- Forgiving that beautiful, vulnerable, and trusting inner child/ adolescent who still resides in the center of your heart
- Awakening to an inner awareness that by *not* healing the child within you, you have the propensity to hurt others in the same way that you were wounded
- Transforming the desire to have or manipulate for sexual con-quest or financial gain/security, thus ending the cycles of abuse and misaligned power that may have been generated by your attempts to fulfill your own unmet needs

When you emotionally disconnect from the damaging wounds of neglect and actually become unconscious of those wounds, a shadow self is created. Instead of using all of your beautiful, innate, intuitive powers for love, healing, and helping others, you are prone to perpe-trate and hurt others. This shadow aspect of Chiron in Taurus longs for the light of love to shine into these wounds with forgiveness, heal-ing, unconditional love, and with authentic connection to your precious inner child and adolescent self.

As all bodies are designed and programmed to respond to physical enjoyment, your body may have physically responded to inappropriate sexual coercion, trauma, or abuse in its naturally designed way of pleasurable arousal.

There is no shame in your body's response to the trauma, abuse, or coercion. There is *no fault* to be found *within you* at all. Forgiving your body and yourself for anything you've held against yourself is key to your complete healing. Gift yourself love for the body that you inhabit and fully restore and reestablish relationships with your *healthy* adult sexuality, finances, and material possessions.

You will benefit greatly by developing skills to meet your own unmet childhood needs. One way is through self-love and self-approval born out of a corrective emotional experience in the context of a therapeutic setting that's supportive and affirming. Being mirrored in this therapeutic alliance will allow you to learn to empathize with yourself and understand how you have been affected and how you affect others with your words and actions.

Your daily self-care practices are important to maintain as a cornerstone of your routines and rituals. Devote yourself and a portion of your time daily to meditation, journal writing, professional work that has deep meaning for you, humanitarian pursuits of service and giving back, spending time with friends, and interacting with an intimate partner who can tell you the truth about his or her experience of you. In these ways a solid foundation is laid for the building of your beautiful self-image based on loving yourself as you truly are. Remember, you were born perfect, and you are worthy of unconditional love no matter what.

Your healing is found through love with commitment. This means that healing is found in your commitment to visiting the wounded places in your memory as the devalued and wounded child you once were.

Your inner child is the conceptualized image of yourself as the innocent young one of a childhood past. It's all of the internalized thoughts, feelings, and experiences of childhood that reside in your adult memory—both conscious memory and subconscious memory.

It's important to become intimately familiar with this little one, and the adolescent self within. Create an image of him/her/them to hold within your mind and heart. When you are triggered and feeling twinges of pain from past wounds of neglect, send unconditional love to these younger parts of yourself.

Invest in the work necessary to strengthen your emotional capacity to be with these emotions. Instead of turning to escapist, numbing, self-harming, and dissociative behaviors, learn to self-soothe in new and healthy ways.

Affirmation work is an important tool that can be used to replace internalized, critical messages from neglectful or abusive caretakers, past or present. Affirmation work involves using a loving narrative of encouragement, empathy, and acceptance of yourself as you are today. Finding a source of deep and unconditional love can't be stressed enough. Forgiving yourself is germane to accessing a radiant white-light shower of peace for your soul. This peace transcends any earthly trappings and is radically different from your former temporary refuges of escape that left you unfulfilled.

Utilizing meditations that contain messages of affirmation permeates your senses and saturates your body, soul, and spirit with new messages of love, safety, security, and trust. This is a powerful combination of tools for growth and healing. Make a commitment of even five minutes a day to participate in guided meditations with affirmations. This work will shift your unconscious and reveal self-sabotaging behaviors and patterns that have hurt you and others.

Another great source of support in sending forgiveness to yourself, and offer amends and atonement to those you may have wounded, is found in the book *Conscious Uncoupling: 5 Steps to Living Happily Even After* by my friend Katherine Woodward Thomas. Called soul-to-soul communication, this process invites you to use your imagination in a meditative state to heal yourself and another person by inviting his or her soul to come and sit in dialogue with yours. It is a powerful healing experience that brings closure and forgiveness to people in your past whom you can no longer speak to in person.

You may find as you begin this healing work that the shadow side of Chiron in Taurus is buried in your unconscious and may manifest in behaviors that incur the unwanted criticism of others, instead of bringing about the desired closeness, understanding, and empathy you wish to receive. These shadow aspects of Chiron in Taurus are a tendency to excuse and justify within yourself overly harsh and critical judgments of others; you may verbalize these thoughts in order to push people away. What may be driving harsh, possibly even cruel words and actions toward others is your fear of vulnerability and intimacy.

This can present itself when acting from your unconscious where you are actually dismissive of others or you seek to dehumanize them in some way. You may have felt stuck in a cycle of judging and dismissing your own self. Beware of your tendency to dehumanize others for self-protection.

If you are reading this and it's resonating with you, please give yourself permission to begin the journey of deep self-forgiveness. It will allow you access to a higher vantage point from which to see yourself and others more clearly. Truly, we are equally valuable and vulnerable human beings, and we all deserve love and forgiveness.

The need to truly hold your inner child tightly with unobstructed and unbridled compassion, understanding, empathy, attunement, and unconditional love is possibly your deepest need. I ask that you consider, right now, granting yourself permission to experience this.

Here's a way you might begin this work. Breathe compassion and understanding into yourself. Try to release yourself from expectations that are self-imposed and unrealistic. Be careful to notice when you're unable to meet your own expectations, because that triggers your internal judgments. Try to enlist your inner moral compass as an accountability partner and supportive inner coach to help yourself achieve this particular challenge. Commit to treating others with more respect and sincerity instead of using your innate charm to manipulate outcomes in your favor.

Most important of all is to remember that you are worthy of unconditional forgiveness and love. You are worthy and deserving, unlike what you may, in the past, have been told by abusive caretakers.

As human beings we are not immune from making mistakes or feeling pain. Both experiences, in fact, are necessary components of growth. The gifts of learning that come to us through hardship are a large part of what we bring to those we serve. Remembering that most people *are* doing the very best that they know how to do. Life *is* for us and not against us. Life is happening *as* us. Unseen forces are at play continually to bring us what we desire. The odds *are* in our favor. Over and over again repeat these supportive messages to yourself. Infuse your work with this energy, your life with this energy, your relationships with this energy.

Think back to the ways you had fun as a child and as an adolescent. In some families, overarching neglect, trauma, abuse, lack of material resources, or the issues present in a single parent home may have dwarfed your childhood development and your carefree adolescence.

It's never too late to give yourself beautiful opportunities to let your inner child and adolescent emerge and be happy now. You can learn to protect, love, laugh, and be with those parts of yourself. Take your healing as an opportunity to expand into your adult self in ways that are both fun and responsible. You deserve this reparenting of yourself.

⮑ *Takeaways*

⚶ If you are a survivor of sexual abuse, coercion, rape, or trauma of any kind, commit to a course of formalized healing. Being loving to yourself and enlisting the assistance of a healing professional will enable you to heal Chiron's core wounds at the deepest level. You owe this to yourself and to those you love. Commit to investing in yourself through the journey of this work.

❧ Commit to identifying one thing a day to appreciate about yourself that doesn't have to do with material success, appearance, or promoting a certain image. Focus on intrinsic qualities such as kindness, patience, generosity, being helpful, being forgiving, or being gentle, for instance.

❧ Actively heal your relationship with your body. You may judge your body harshly and may have suffered from an eating disorder or eating-disordered thinking and ensuing detrimental patterns. Before turning to cosmetic surgery, with love and acceptance, consider embracing the idea that the body you are in is the perfect body for your soul and your spirit. It truly is, and you are beautiful as you are.

❧ Commit to changing the pattern of using your sexuality for power or as an escape. Instead, use sexuality in a sacred context to create, connect, and heal. Make amends where needed with persons from the past that have been hurt by your misuse of sexuality.

❧ Affirmations

"I love and approve of myself just as I am."
"I allow myself to heal."
"I am lovable."
"I am good enough now."
"I forgive all others, including myself."

K8

Chiron in Gemini

Core Wounding in Empathetic Attunement

Wounded Chiron Feels

Overly intellectual

Caught in self-destructive
thoughts

Not seen or heard

Healed Chiron Feels

Heart centered

An ability to express feelings
through words

Integrated

Authentic

Prince Harry, duke of Sussex; Lady Gaga; Rihanna; Katy Perry; and the Fourteenth Dalai Lama all have Chiron in the sign of Gemini. Each of them is an example of an individual who has successfully transformed the psychoastrology of their core wounding. They have become public figures who have learned to authentically express themselves in their respective fields. As such, they are in turn valued and respected for what they do, and are empathetically heard, which are two of the deepest needs for a Chiron in Gemini individual.

The millennials born with Chiron in Gemini are a widely diverse group who express themselves by adopting personas ranging from Goths to Wall Street hustlers, from activists to conservatives. Through authentic self-expression, Chiron in Gemini's wounds are transformed and healed. What does this mean for *you* as an individual with Chiron in Gemini?

The experience of empathetic attunement is a necessary developmental milestone of childhood that exists in order for us to develop the ability to identify and express our feelings verbally. With Chiron in Gemini, the ability to fully develop one's interpersonal communication skills may have been delayed or arrested as a result of not being seen or heard in a kind, considerate, and compassionate way. Simply put, a painful outcome of this placement is the childhood experience of being perennially misunderstood. As a young person, your caregivers' lack of attunement to your various emotional states may have caused a disruption in your ability to communicate effectively.

You may have been criticized, ridiculed, or shamed by an authority figure, which resulted in low self-worth and low self-esteem. As a byproduct, you are prone to devaluing and comparing yourself to others, which results in the generation of negative feelings about yourself. As you pursue your goals, this form of self-sabotage can undermine your forward momentum. Instead of being valued and respected for the wisdom and knowledge you possess, you may experience being misperceived personally and professionally, and feel that you're not good enough.

Even though comparing yourself to others is something you engage in often, it's a losing game. At any given moment of time there are always (in our perception) people doing "better" or "more" than we are, and there are always (in our perception) people doing "worse" or "less" than we are. Instead of placing some people above and others below oneself, accepting your differences and respective strengths can help you view yourself in accurate relationship with others. Developing your abilities and pursuing your own unique gifts can help you develop a relationship to your own best noncompetitive self.

Cultivating the space within your consciousness to accept where you are right now, and embracing who you are in the here and now, is significant for your healing and sustained well-being. Learning to tune in to the present moment with mindful acceptance and gratitude for *what is* can be helpful to get off the hamster wheel of comparison. Each of us is here to create our own unique path. Indeed, *A Course in Miracles* talks about each of us having a "highly individualized curriculum." We contribute our own individualized verse to the "collective's song" by adding our authentic voice.

In terms of the issue of comparing ourselves to others, when we struggle with this, a better question to ask is, "Am I a better version of myself today than yesterday? Last week? Last month? Last year?" And finally, "Whom do I want to become? Whom am I growing into with the decisions I am making today?"

Another facet of core wounding that affects one's concept of self is when you think others are smarter, are wittier, or know more than you do. It may be that you were made to feel less adequate than your peers by being criticized, made fun of, being the class clown, or being bullied in a school setting.

Alienation and bullying between you and a sibling leaves a wound that was no doubt created when you were young, and may be maintained into adulthood. If you are an only child, you may have faced feelings of anxiety and loneliness, with uncertainty about how to emotionally connect with others.

As an adult, your early memory imprints (that resulted in low self-esteem and self-worth) can manifest as disruptions in your attempts to connect with others using your inner compass and guidance.

You might feel challenged in the verbal expression of your true self;

therefore, you may find yourself in situations where you seldom speak up for yourself, and don't discuss your needs and desires. Conversely, you may overcompensate for this perceived deficiency by way of compulsive talking. This behavior works to hide your feelings of fear and the shame of not knowing how to accurately and comfortably express your thoughts, feelings, experiences, and desires.

Learning to accurately identify and express your needs verbally allows you to shift and break self-defeating patterns so that you may then be authentically heard by others. Feeling the deep relief of being seen and reflected empathetically provides healing to the wounded inner child who previously felt invisible. Your transformation is found by expressing your own unique perspective to others. Say "yes" to these opportunities and experiences, for they are the foundation of your new identity.

Another key to healing from the experiences surrounding a lack of empathetic attunement is learning, in the present, the skills necessary to be able to empathetically attune to yourself. We heal *through* the resolution of our wounds, not over, under, or around them. It's always exciting to notice your own progress as you let go of old communication patterns and grow in new and healthy directions.

Being empathetically attuned to yourself means, first, that you are aware of how you are feeling, and second, that you speak and act in genuine alignment with how you really feel. At times this may require verbally sharing your thoughts and feelings with the individuals surrounding you. It can help to begin this practice with a trusted individual who is available to assist you in making these small shifts in self-attunement and communication. This individual may be a trusted friend, healing practitioner, romantic partner, sibling, parent, or colleague. This individual can help you to identify and process what you truly think and feel, even when what you have to say may be upsetting or rock the boat in some way. In fact, it may be the case that the more vulnerable your statements are, the more powerful this transformative work may be, for it is in these extreme experiences that we grow the most exponentially.

Practice with those closest to you first, then experiment with people whom you perceive to be more challenging. This gentle, mindful practice of communicating your differences with others will help you gain confidence in yourself.

Taking appropriate action on your own behalf so that your authentic self can be in charge of the social and professional arenas of your life will become easier and more natural over time. With each passing interaction, your self-confidence will be boosted in long-lasting ways.

In my research and experience, the core wounding of individuals with Chiron in Gemini is directly correlated to one's current attachment style. This means that the degree to which you have developed a secure attachment within yourself is the degree to which you feel comfortable expressing yourself in the world. Again, the three categories of attachment styles are secure, avoidant, and anxious. Please review your particular attachment style by revisiting the discussion about attachment styles found in chapter 4 beginning on page 61.

The shadow side of Chiron in Gemini may be buried in your unconscious and manifest in behaviors or communication patterns that incur the unwanted criticism of others, instead of bringing about the desired understanding, empathy, and outcome that you wish to receive. A few potential blind spots for you to become aware of include lecturing others or being overly boisterous, even obnoxious. In contrast to communicating appropriately, unhealed Chiron in Gemini prompts us to speak too loudly and in a manner that repels people rather than drawing them into conversation. People might describe you as a know-it-all.

Taking steps to change communication habits by learning new delivery dynamics will allow others to feel close to you. To confront these patterns in a supportive and gentle environment that mirrors respect for you, I recommend therapy, coaching, public speaking class, or similar professional activities, up to and including a healing practitioner. It's helpful to procure a productive setting in which to address the personal issues associated with these behaviors. It's important that you feel safe enough to expose your feelings and concerns, and know that they will be addressed with curiosity, empathy, and support instead of judgment and criticism.

ම *Takeaways*

- Before speaking to a person or group, take a moment to collect your thoughts and clearly identify in your mind what needs to be said. Then take the risk to speak that authentic truth in a respectful, polite, yet assured tone of voice.

- Ask a person you trust to practice authentic communication with you. Agree to follow ground rules such as mutual respect; one person speaks at a time; there is no right or wrong; this is a safe space in which to make mistakes; and so on. By engaging in this process you will develop proficiency in your communication skills, which will become easier and more comfortable over time.

- Practice listening—without thinking about your response— while the other person is talking. Truly be in the moment with that person. This is the practice of *active listening* utilizing *mindful* presence. As you focus on listening to the person speaking, you will learn to engage in spontaneous, meaningful dialogue. This new communication practice will be deeply gratifying to you and for others as well.

ම **Affirmations**

"I am seen and heard."

"I give myself permission to be authentic."

"I speak my truth."

"I am empowered to be my true self."

"I attract people who want to be with me."

"I am loved."

K9

Chiron in Cancer

Core Wounding by Abandonment

Wounded Chiron Feels

Abandoned

Unlovable

Unresolved grief

Suicidal ideation

Healed Chiron Feels

A secure sense of home

Nurturing

Self-love from the inner

mother

Let's begin our exploration of Chiron in Cancer by recalling historic events that occurred under this influence. These events demonstrate the transformation of core wounding by abandonment into experiences of being nurtured and establishing a sense of belonging. In February of 1990, Nelson Mandela was released from prison after spending twenty-seven years behind bars. He beautifully reframed his experience of incarceration by choosing to teach us about liberation from the imprisonment of our own minds.

The Communist Party of the Soviet Union voted to end its monopoly of power in 1991. This cleared the way for multiparty elections. In this, we saw that country moving toward a more inclusive way of governing. This demonstrates the healing potential of the core wound of Chiron in Cancer, which had been inflicted by the previous system. How is your psychoastrology affected as an individual with this placement? If you are an individual with Chiron in the sign of Cancer, your core wounding occurred during childhood in your family system of relationships. Due to your home environment being unsafe, threatening, insecure, or dangerous in some way, the end results were that you experienced abandonment and felt unlovable.

These experiences caused an inner displacement for you. You didn't develop a sense of home as a secure base. This innate insecurity may today be causing you to struggle to find where you belong, where to plant roots, and where to create a home.

Not knowing where you belong leads to a sense of detachment from your instincts and intuition. In order to compensate, you may sacrifice your own needs in order to be a part of a relationship, group, or community.

Your core wound of abandonment is transformed and healed by creating and then connecting with the spirit of a loving mother. This loving mother resides within you and embraces the truth of your innate lovability.

By planting deep roots of nourishing, supportive love for yourself (based in messages of affirmation that love is found within and home is anywhere you lay your head), you can experience a deeper sense of connection to home as a safe place. The creation of home as a safe and secure place is a cornerstone, or building block, from which we launch into the world, and then return to for replenishment, nourishment, and rest.

When I think of the core wounding of Chiron in Cancer, the primary work is to heal from loss and grief. It may be that you need to explore the loss of what, as a child, was not there to begin with and therefore you did not receive. Other needs not met may have been the safety you craved or the love you needed or the comfort you longed for and never attained. These are just a few types of loss you now have the opportunity to grieve and heal.

Earlier we referenced Dr. Elisabeth Kübler-Ross and her five stages of grief, as well as David Kessler's expansion on this and my offering designed to assist you in healing from grief with a psychospiritual approach that includes utilizing the chakra system alongside the stages of grief model (see pages 69–75). Take some time to turn back to this section and view your core wounding by abandonment through both of these lenses.

My intention is that you find compassion for yourself as the child and adolescent you once were—a child who may have had to cope with circumstances and events well beyond your developmental capacity to manage. Now is the time for you to develop the inner emotional and spiritual musculature to empathetically attend to your abandonment wounds. You deserve to be loved, and therefore, you can create a support system now.

The shadow side of Chiron in Cancer may be hidden through unconscious patterns and manifest in behaviors that incur the unwanted judgment of others, instead of bringing about the desired closeness and empathy you wish to receive. For the Chiron in Cancer individual, others may view you as moody because you may internalize your feelings of insecurity or uncertainty instead of verbalizing them. Or you may close yourself off from life entirely and isolate. You may be overly self-protective or hypersensitive to life. Or you may feel so entirely alone and unimportant that you may contemplate taking your own life.

If this is where you are as you read this, please immediately reach out for help by calling 911, a hospital emergency room, or a trusted individual. Seeking treatment with a healing professional can help you to deconstruct the walls that keep you from feeling connected. My intention for you is that over time you will feel deeply plugged in to an inner well of love that is available, and is strengthened through bonds you will form with others. I myself have had suicidal feelings and thoughts; I once contemplated taking my own life. I had to dig deep, and blindly consider that I was experiencing an illusion in my own consciousness. The despair I felt obstructed the love that others had for me. Over time, with the help of a healing professional, I learned to love myself. Please give yourself this chance. I stand with you and am here for you.

∂ *Takeaways*

- Spend time clearing clutter. . . . Donate or sell items you don't need or use anymore. To any degree possible at this time, make your home an *oasis*. To whatever degree possible, create a living space of comfort that reflects your personality. Revisit this decluttering process twice a year, or more frequently—for instance, with the changing of the seasons. Energy flows more freely through spaces that have room for its flow. Depleting emotions hang around stagnant and congested spaces. Ask for help from family and friends, or hire a housekeeper to assist you. Maintaining your home will help you feel more connected to it in a positive way that energizes you.

- To begin pairing good memories with home, invite people into your space once a month. Have a potluck, play games, watch movies, or host a book club. A *house* becomes a *home* when it is filled with love and laughter. Hosting other people also helps you stay accountable to maintaining the order and cleanliness of your living space. It's not cheating! It's enlisting others as your accountability partners.

ᨭ Join a group, team, or club; form your own; or look online for new ways to connect with others. One website that I like and use often is Meetup.com. Research community message boards at coffee shops or churches. Or ask around about ways to meet and connect with others who share a mutual interest, hobby, or passion.

ᨬ Affirmations

"I trust myself to be at home wherever I am."
"I'm creating a home of love."
"I am my own home."
"I am safe."
"I value myself."
"I am important."

10

Chiron in Leo

....

Core Wounding in Creativity

Wounded Chiron Feels

Self-critical or conversely
    boastful

A tendency toward
    self-sabotage

Healed Chiron Feels

Passionately creative

Productive

Playful

Romantic

L et's begin our exploration with two historical events that were influenced by the shadow side of Chiron in Leo, which can intimidate by brute force when unconscious and unregulated. We see this poignantly in the opening of the Nazi extermination camps Bełżec, Sobibór, and Treblinka II in 1942. In those camps 1,444,508 Jewish people were murdered. In another example, in 1992, with Chiron in Leo, justice was not served when a jury acquitted four LAPD officers accused of excessive force in the videotaped beating of African-American motorist Rodney King in Los Angeles.

We see both the psychoastrological wounding and healing potential of Chiron in Leo with the millennials born under this placement. In a mixed blessing, the millennial generation is responsible for the creation of social media sites including Facebook, Instagram, and Snapchat, and the phenomenon of selfies. While these platforms allow us to interact more easily, they have also contributed to feelings of depression, anxiety, and the social isolation that can lead to suicide. Let's look at what the psychoastrology of Chiron in Leo means for you as an individual.

The healing potential of individuals with Chiron in the sign of Leo resides in your ability to access your creativity. You actually have within you the innate potential to *embody* creativity and leave a powerful legacy. However, you may feel obstructed from feeling connected to your muse. This particular blockage also affects your ability to maintain success in your work and personal relationships, both platonic and romantic.

Have no worry, for your release is merely temporarily tucked away underneath self-criticism awaiting the ointment of empathy to awaken and inspire your creative musings. Your healing entails the administration of large doses of self-compassion and understanding to your own good self.

You have a tendency to judge yourself harshly, at the same time encouraging others to be uniquely creative. This is disempowering for you because you love being recognized for your creative abilities. When your ability to manifest is blocked or thwarted, you may feel like something is wrong with you.

As a child in school you may have been criticized for approaching projects in a different way from your peers. You were one of those young people who were usually thinking outside of the box, and therefore criticized for being different. So although you were never doing anything wrong, you may have felt as if you were. More than likely, you didn't receive enough encouragement and praise for being the uniquely creative person that you were and no doubt still are. Today increasing numbers of schools are developing outlets for children to express their creativity. They are being increasingly nurtured according to their own particular learning styles.

Healing for individuals with Chiron in the sign of Leo comes by giving yourself permission to create for fun, and to experience pleasure and enjoyment through play. Healing also happens when you allow yourself to express your authentic desires in the arenas of romance, family, and work. Creating joy in your work, in your intimate relationships, and with your family and friends will transform past experiences of struggle to ones of fulfillment wherein you feel a sense of accomplishment and connection—even mastery.

One methodology available to support you in this quest is the use of affirmations to shift or replace self-critical internal messages. Affirmations work in conjunction with guided meditation that is focused on self-love and forgiveness. This will accelerate your process of learning to love yourself deeply, from the inside out. As mentioned earlier, I personally use and recommend to my clients the guided meditations offered by The Honest Guys, Abraham-Hicks, the Chopra Center, and many others, all of which can be accessed online and which are also referenced in the resources section of this book.

As a result of having Chiron in Leo, you can be privately or publicly self-deprecating and harbor low self-esteem. You are critical of yourself for not knowing how to grow and expand your creative endeavors. Sometimes you may sabotage the manifestation of your own dreams and desires in favor of nurturing another's dream or being a fantastic cheerleader for your children, romantic or business partners, friends, or parents. All the while you may be neglecting yourself and your own endeavors.

Your healing entails honoring the inner calling of creating passionately for yourself. For you, healing Chiron's core wounds means expressing your soul's desire through art, music, writing, performance, charity work, activism, or business endeavors. Do not stop short of achieving your desires by overserving the needs of others. It's important that you learn to develop balance.

It can be fulfilling to explore what your own passionate needs actually are and to develop a plan to meet them. Giving these unexplored parts of yourself a voice, or an expression, or a vehicle to articulate your unexpressed desires will mobilize your psychoastrological healing.

Your drive toward wholeness and liberation is held in the fulfillment of your own creative longings. Look for ways in the past when you were living by the default settings of old and outdated thinking patterns. Then today, imagine consciously directing your free will with choices you can begin to make from a place of empowerment. Begin each morning by setting intentions to prepave your day by grounding yourself. Declare and intend that creativity, love, and joy will flow forth in everything that is to manifest that day.

A question to ask yourself as you begin each day and look ahead to the week is, "Am I overcommitted, or do I need to change my plans so I'll be available to explore what really makes me happy?" Develop a version of this question that suits your own voice. This is going to aid you in prepaving your future with foresight and intention.

Use your vivid imagination to envision how you want your future to feel. Really take some time to feel into the imagery that looks like the life you want. Begin to set limits and boundaries with others so that you can prioritize yourself first.

In the past you may have created using disempowered and default thinking patterns based in prioritizing the well-being of others at your expense. As you begin to identify and participate in the people, places, and things that delight you, while disengaging with what depletes you, self-efficacy and self-confidence result.

Work to shift your thoughts from self-judgment based in fear and lack to thoughts of self-affirmation based in acceptance and abundance. With this remodeling you can now make changes easily by using your witty humor, daft mind, and intellectual abilities; these same abilities you may have muted in the past, all the while thinking that in doing so others would feel more comfortable. You can now choose to stop making others comfortable at your own expense. It does not serve you anymore. Through the self-validation methods I have suggested, it's time to step into your powerful, authentic self.

Though you usually don't make it known, except to those very trusted and close to you, validation is important to you. You have a vulnerable underbelly that is supersensitive and wants to be nurtured and loved. You are a gentle soul who needs and loves admiration.

A key to Chiron in Leo is to learn to carve out the space and time for your own endeavors, which will allow your light to shine. In fully pursuing and embodying your creativity, you become an example for others that then models the fact that it's okay for them to do the same. I borrow this sentiment in a quote by Marianne Williamson, from her book *A Return to Love*,

Our deepest fear is not that we are inadequate. Our deepest fear is that we are powerful beyond measure. It is our light, not our darkness that most frightens us. We ask ourselves, who am I to be brilliant, gorgeous, talented, fabulous? Actually, who are you *not* to be? You are a child of God. Your playing small does not serve the world. There is nothing enlightened about shrinking so that other people won't feel insecure around you. We are all meant to shine, as children do. We were born to make manifest the glory of God that is within us. It's not just in some of us; it's in everyone. And as we let our own light shine, we unconsciously give other people permission to do the same. As we are liberated from our own fear, our presence automatically liberates others.

What a gift you are! What a brightly lit example you are when you take action to follow your own bliss. Tune into your own inner heart, mind, and spirit; follow the bright lamp deep within you that lights your path. If you have children, be an exemplary model of self-confidence for them by finding the sources of your own happiness. If you don't have children, be the best example of authenticity that you can be for those in your sphere of influence. We're all looking for permission to be our authentic selves, and you are a leader to show us the way.

The shadow side of Chiron in Leo may be buried in your unconscious and hidden patterns or thoughts and can manifest in behaviors that trigger the unwanted judgment and criticism of others, instead of bringing about the desired understanding and empathy you wish to receive from them. As a Chiron in Leo individual, you are criticized when you compensate for feelings of lack by acting out in hurtful ways that are perceived as being negative, boastful, haughty, and perhaps even bullying. You may be known for intimidating others by force. The negative attention you receive will, more than likely, unconsciously reinforce the self-critical beliefs you hold about yourself. Please know that you can change and transform this self-sabotaging pattern and these tendencies.

Your core wounds need loving attention and have not yet received that attention. Let's bring the shadow aspects of your core wounds to the light of love and forgiveness. This kind of work can be compared to working a new muscle group that you weren't aware of in the past. That muscle group now lets you know of its presence through soreness or pain. The soreness following exercise is actually evidence that what you did was beneficial. Your physical discomfort confirms that you are on the right path. The same applies to psychological growth and development.

You may experience some resistance from others as you exercise and use your new skills. Quite simply, you are showing up for yourself differently, and others may not like it. Their displeasure does not mean that you are offtrack.

Drop into the guidance system of your own body to assess if you are accurately and empathetically responding from your core self. Look carefully at the ways you need to be heard, seen, and mirrored. If you are not being heard, seen, and mirrored, then you may decide to have a heart-to-heart with those concerned. They may indeed be giving you pushback or friction for changing the way you are now in relationship with yourself. It may help to articulate the ways you have organized and conducted your life up to this point, and then verbalize how you are changing your patterns.

It may also help to share with these trusted individuals your desired outcomes and goals and ask if, instead of resisting you, they might support you in making these shifts. Asking for support as you step out in new ways may be all it takes to shift these relationships and preserve them anew.

Others in your life may not have been aware of the depletion or unhappiness you may have been feeling, given that your powerful personality can flawlessly cover your underlying dissatisfaction. And they may have been unaware of the mask that you have been wearing to hide behind. This mask of bravado that you may have been wearing you can now remove.

In order to create the legacy you are capable of offering, being authentically creative and passionate is important. Leaving a legacy is not something you just do at the time of your physical demise. Begin to think about the legacy you want to leave as you walk out of a room, hang up from a phone call, or move through loss or disappointment.

We leave these little legacies every day in some way: in how we communicate with others, say hello or goodbye, or handle a stressful situation. Becoming aware of this process gives you lots of options to consider, which previously you may not have been aware of. Use your sense of humor to make this paradigm shift authentic and creative for yourself and those who depend on you. Each day look for an opportunity to leave a legacy that you feel good about. Be proud. In this way your unique bright light beams from your courageous heart, warming those around you in beautiful and inspiring ways.

❧ *Takeaways*

- To give yourself a regularly scheduled time to access and express your creativity, take a creative class (art, music, design, sewing, etc.). You can also do this at home by diving into a coloring book, making art, listening to or making music, cooking, baking, or DIY projects, for instance. Try different things to see what sticks!

- In order to have adequate time to prepare for the next day or plan for your week, arrange to arrive at work early or stay late several days a week. Set limits with others to prioritize your self-care. Meeting your goals while maintaining your own emotional well-being in this way leads to feelings of power and success.

- Make yourself available to help a coworker, child, friend, partner, or family member with a project in a way that feels good. This will aid in the co-creation of a shared goal and build or strengthen a meaningful relationship.

❧ *Affirmations*

"I live to create."

"I create what didn't exist."

"I am unique."

"I am powerful."

"I can prioritize myself."

"I can come first."

K11

Chiron in Virgo

Core Wounding in Managing Physical Health and Routines

Wounded Chiron Feels

Broken

Unable to cope

Neglectful of one's self-care

Hypochondriac

Healed Chiron Feels

Self-nurturing

An ability to follow healthy
routines

An ability to have fun

Joyful

In 1995 under the influence of Chiron in Virgo, the World Trade Organization (WTO) was formed to monitor U.S. international trade decisions. Our government's proactive shift to protect and stimulate the health of our economy, while providing boundaries for us to have productive trade relations with other countries by establishing the WTO, exemplifies the healing of Chiron in the sign of Virgo during that transit. The core wounding to our country at that time had to do with neglected and insufficient boundaries that were a threat to the safety of U.S. trade relations.

Generation Z kids born with Chiron in Virgo have, on the one hand, grown up in a highly sophisticated media and computer culture, yet have underdeveloped face-to-face interpersonal social skills as a result. Healing this generation's psychoastrology will be found through developing and maintaining healthy interpersonal connections. What does Chiron in Virgo mean for you personally?

If Chiron is in the sign of Virgo in your natal chart, your core wounding affects all of the aspects surrounding your physical health and the establishment (and maintenance) of healthy routines. Your personal and professional lives may be out of balance and feel overwhelming to you. You may experience moments of thinking you are somehow broken. Yet you are unsure of what to do or how to heal. This causes you some mental confusion and emotional turmoil.

You are known to have a dedication to service and love for teaching and healing, combined with a revolutionary spirit. This is positive! Also working in your favor is that Chiron has a natural affinity for the sign of Virgo and feels at home here. This is because Chiron is the embodiment of self-healing. Therefore, Chiron in Virgo begs you to grow in the areas of your personal health, self-healing, and the maintenance of those routines. Ask him to help and guide you in these areas.

Because you are such a dependable provider, teacher, partner, parent, employee, and friend, the uncertainty you experience about not knowing what to do to help yourself is deeply disturbing to you. The key to your healing is found in learning to nurture yourself. This encompasses the consumption of good food, getting enough sleep, and the physical enjoyment of exercise, adventure, and pleasure, including sex.

It's important to know your limitations (it's okay to have them), because by setting limits you transcend maladaptive coping mechanisms that you may be suffering from, including restrictive dieting, addictive habits, or workaholic tendencies.

Deep down you have known that routines that leave you depleted from overworking are neither healthy nor sustainable. And you understand that there is a deeper issue at hand. You don't like to disappoint your loved ones, and you fear that if you take the time to care for yourself you might let them down, so you keep pushing through, ever hoping to catch a break.

What I want you to let into your consciousness right now is that your loved ones *want* you to be happy, healthy, and refreshed every day. They don't want you to be depleted and empty. When you are scraping the bottom of the barrel, you, like anyone else in this predicament, are raw, edgy, easily agitated, and exhausted.

I know that you *intellectually* understand the importance of self-care; however, you overlook and neglect your own needs, violating your inner knowing of what it means to care for yourself. Conversely, you will voluntarily make yourself available to help others. Burnout is on the horizon, if you are not there already.

If there is an imbalance between output and input, that disparity over time will be damaging to every system of your body. The deeper issue is centered on the unfortunate belief that if you give and give and give, then you will feel good about yourself and, in turn, be loved and valued by others.

You may believe that doing for others is how you referee self-criticism and judgment, and thereby compensate for feelings of low self-esteem. Defense mechanisms such as sublimation and compensation work temporarily, giving you a false sense of happiness and security.

You are able to heal your psychoastrology and come back into alignment by learning to set boundaries and self-validate. This is accomplished by restructuring your routines to include adequate rest, nourishment, healthy exercise, fun, joy, and pleasure. Enjoy your productivity, which can include meaningful ways to be of service that energize you instead of depleting you.

A place to begin insourcing self-approval is by implementing a daily practice of identifying qualities that you genuinely like about yourself. Say them aloud, write them down, and add to the list daily if possible. Over time these seeds will grow into generous doses of self-love and acceptance and will feed your inner garden.

As you regularly give voice to what you approve of about yourself, this self-affirmation practice becomes an energizing force in your life. This practice of acknowledging yourself facilitates a fundamental paradigm shift from a focus on what is lacking to a focus on what you appreciate. This consciousness shift will bring more positivity and levity into your life. You are creating a foundation to build on by maintaining this daily gratitude practice. We actually learn more quickly and with longer-lasting effects through encouragement than through criticism. Our teachers, schools, family, peers, culture, and the media have told us the opposite, but research shows otherwise.

One such paradigm is a coaching mind-set approach taken from a strength-based model. I recall this perspective from my undergraduate years in the 1990s. Although people do not usually know they are drawing from this model, it is widely used today in life coaching, psychotherapy, counseling, personnel management, executive coaching, and energy healing.

The strength-based model is a social work practice theory that emphasizes an individual's self-determination and strengths. It's a philosophy that views people as being resourceful and resilient in the face of adversity.

To begin applying the model right now and shift into healthier routines immediately, take out a paper and pen, and let's complete the following inventory. Set a timer for fifteen minutes and write out a list of your strengths, which include all of the qualities you like about yourself.

Some examples may be all of the ways you enjoy helping people by being of service to others at work, home, and play. It may be the resilience you have developed over the years in your chosen career. It may be the way you are able to keep people organized and on track with their goals. Make an exhaustive inventory, knowing that you can always add to this list as you develop additional insight and awareness.

Once you have completed an exhaustive list, go back through it and put a star next to the strengths that may deplete you, even though those strengths appear to be beneficial (at face value). Examples of what strengths might be depleting you may be some of the ways you sacrifice for others. For instance, at the expense of your own responsibilities, you may stay up late to help your partner or child with a project on deadline. Keep going down your list, and place stars next to the strengths that also keep you from adequately maintaining your own health and well-being.

Now let's get creative by adjusting some of your perceived strengths so that you can maximize your energy and desire to be of service without compromising your health. We want to augment the ways you are prone to denying yourself the basic things that you need to be and stay healthy.

Self-neglect and deprivation can be dangerous to your health when left untreated. In response to the starred items on your list, some potential solutions would be, for example, to consider letting that person know that staying up late to help him or her with a project deadline leaves you feeling depleted and unable to address the responsibilities you face in the morning.

Ask if there is another time, or another person, whom they could ask for help instead. Often others closest to you are not aware that the help you freely offer also depletes you. So this exercise is really all about looking for ways to set boundaries for yourself.

To conserve energy for your own healing goals, setting boundaries is necessary. You may have derived your self-esteem entirely from being of service to others. Identifying new ways to self-validate, without giving so much of yourself, will help you create inwardly sourced self-esteem.

Maybe you can begin to delegate to others around you some of the tasks you've been taking care of by yourself. Maybe you can enlist the help of someone who will champion the nuts and bolts components of an event so you can focus on other activities that might give you more flexibility in your schedule.

Instead of completing every component of an event yourself, perhaps others could work to find and secure funding for the event, and could promote the event. Or you may enjoy the more detailed work of a project, so delegate management duties to someone else. If that is the case, you can complete your portion of responsibility and leave others to their tasks.

By shifting your responsibilities and delegating to others, you open up space in your calendar and establish routines to look after your mental, physical, and spiritual health in ways that your core wound has prevented you from doing before.

With Chiron in Virgo, your core wounding also affects your belief system as it pertains to balancing your health and well-being and associated maintenance routines. Looking for solutions through the lens of a new paradigm, such as the strength-based perspective, could be a helpful and practical exercise you can try for yourself. Additionally, by bringing your entire household on board, you will be able to more consistently maintain the changes that you have identified and are implementing.

Since you don't live in a vacuum, it can help to share what you need with others in order to be happier and healthier. Individuals who love and support you will want you to take care of your health. As part of the plan to care for yourself, enlist individuals to help you with accountability. Again, we need trusted individuals in our lives to be our accountability partners; they act as touchstones for us. Reach out to them, and let them know that you would like to have them be part of your support team.

If left untreated, the hidden shadow aspects of your core wounding can cause you to act in ways that trigger ridicule and criticism from others, instead of the sensitivity and understanding from them that we desire. The Chiron in Virgo individual can be excessively concerned about his or her personal health and daily routines to the point of hypochondria. Hypochondria is defined as an abnormal anxiety about one's health, especially an unwarranted fear that you have a serious disease. This can drive people away from you instead of drawing them in. Seek proper medical and mental health treatment to cope with fears, worry, and hypochondria.

Another potentially unconscious shadow aspect of the core wounding of Chiron in Virgo is that you may be a serious workaholic. You may recognize that, to the exclusion of other responsibilities, you are out of balance and simply trying to put out fires to stabilize the various areas of your everyday life and routines. You spend a disproportionate time at work. Both the health risks and a host of documented chronic health issues can be the result of physical neglect, coupled with stress brought on by overwork.

To establish a healthy baseline for yourself, try working with various professionals to treat either hypochondria or stress-related health disorders caused by overwork. It's important to hold yourself within a framework of compassion and loving kindness. There is no place for judgments or criticisms as you begin your healing work. Unconditional love can serve as a healing balm for grounding you in the sensation of health and well-being. Allow yourself a supported and gentle place to land mentally and emotionally as you address your behaviors and begin to lay the foundation of your healing journey.

❧ Takeaways

- Invest in a daily planner or online calendar to chart out each week's responsibilities, deadlines, health appointments, *and* playtimes for social and physical activities for *yourself.*

꙳ Schedule your yearly routine health and wellness appointments in advance, and then attend them. Schedule, in advance, babysitting or other household support so that you can keep your scheduled appointments.

꙳ Schedule at least one day off per week. Plan an activity or sleep in and have a lazy day or make arrangements to be with others. Schedule a yearly vacation, even if it's a day trip or a weekend drive to a nearby beach or hiking trail. Take the vacation to whatever degree possible with the intention of taking longer periods of time away when you are able to. A day hike can expand over time to a weekend at Yosemite National Park, for example. With the proper planning and commitment to developing this area of self-care, why not expand your time away to a week or more?!

ᕲ *Affirmations*

"I can be flexible."
"I am healthy and whole."
"I can have balance."
"I am creating a life of balance."
"I allow time for myself, and time for others."
"I allow for imperfections."

K12

Chiron in Libra

Core Wounding in Personal Independence

Wounded Chiron Feels

An underdeveloped sense
of self

Codependency

Healed Chiron Feels

Artistic

Expressive

Creative

The psychoastrology of Chiron in Libra represents the shift from a disempowered identity to one that is strong and has flexible yet protective boundaries. This Chiron in Libra influence was demonstrated when the U.S. government initiated international policy by taking proactive steps to increase our country's presence through attending the UN General Assembly meeting in 1946. In similar fashion, to protect government intelligence, President Harry S. Truman established the CIA in 1947. Both of these historical events demonstrate the healing potential of Chiron in Libra's core wounding by first defining what is needed, expressively articulating those needs, and then putting the necessary mechanisms in place to execute them.

Here are some important questions to ask yourself if you have Chiron in Libra. Do you feel a sense of lack in the development of your personal independence? Do you feel alone and undervalued when you are not in an intimate relationship? When you *are* in an intimate relationship, do you struggle with an underdeveloped sense of your core identity that leads you to sacrifice your true opinions and needs in order to maintain that relationship? Are you pained by wondering how to maintain boundaries between your true self and your relationship self?

Individuals with Chiron in Libra are challenged at a deep level of the heart. You are perceived as kind, loving, fair, and nonconfrontational. You truly enjoy the joy and stability that domestic life brings. At one time the abdication of your sense of self to another may have felt emotionally safe and comforting for you. Perhaps now it is not. As you unpack all of the ways you were taught to defer your power to others, perhaps now is the time to change your intentions and allow yourself to evolve with gentleness and empathy.

Your sense of identity has come primarily from another person instead of your self-definition or the internal prompting of your own unique needs and desires. You possess a vast internal capacity to express yourself, which may be untapped at best and, at the extreme end of the spectrum, blocked. Perhaps there has been a romanticizing of relationships, both platonic and intimate, that does not, in fact, align with the reality of those relationships.

The most expansive intimate relationship and friendships for you will be with individuals who want to get to know what *you* enjoy, what makes *you* happy, and how they can be a part of *your* happiness. You are best suited in choosing a partner who is patient, allowing you the time and space you need to feel secure enough with them to verbalize or show them what you like. They will allow you to direct the relationship when you want to take on that role.

First you must do the work necessary to unearth what your interests and proclivities are so that you can initiate and share them with your partner and with others. Learning the skills to redefine how you view and then enter into relationships is a key aspect of this healing work.

The issues facing the individual with Chiron in Libra remind me of my own work with codependency and my subsequent healing from it. There is something so dreamy and alluring about being attracted to someone, then curling up in the warm safety of their embrace, and finally merging your identity with theirs through lovemaking. We find the outward illusion of feeling safe and comforted, and we are promised that we will never have to struggle on our own again . . . because this beautiful person fulfills the yearning of our core wound, which is to feel protected and loved.

Like many of us, I've experienced fleeting moments of this, and I thought I was complete and whole. Without judgment or criticism, I understand our human desire for this kind of relationship. The one-ness we feel with another is the closest feeling we can simulate to being enveloped in the womb as a developing baby, a memory imprint we all carry in our collective consciousness. In the past I romanticized the other person/partner and assigned them the role of filling the empty holes of my neediness. I learned through the painful ending of friend-ships and relationships that I alone have to fill in my deep inner spaces with self-appreciation, fulfillment, approval, and love.

What I now know to be true, as you probably do also, is that when this type of relationship ends, we are left to soothe and comfort our-selves, alone once again. It's hard and painful to experience such deep comfort from another person and then experience their disconnection.

I'm no stranger to loss, and even as I write this segment of the book,

I reflect back to times when I had that warm embrace of a love that seemed to fulfill me. In those moments I didn't have to soothe or comfort myself; it was so much easier when comfort came from another person. Or so I thought.

Take a moment to be with any memory coming up for you right now. Send yourself love, and if it feels good, send that person you are recalling love also. This can complete that circle to bring you inner peace and resolution. Release the pain, and replace it with gratitude.

It seems almost unfair that we have to both comfort ourselves in life and be strong on our own. Where and why we stumble is due to our own interpretation of events. Our fortune or misfortune is sourced in our ability to read someone accurately (discernment) and then to act accordingly on our own behalf (taking aligned action). How many times have you initially met a potential love interest and then, as you opened your heart to the hope that your deepest emotional and physical needs would finally be fulfilled in that partnership, they suddenly acted in a way that was incongruent with how they'd initially presented themselves?

As a woman in a partnership, I want both my feelings cherished and my thoughts valued. It's not too much for us to ask for this. However, you might have done exactly what I have in the past. You quickly dismiss a partner's, or potential partner's, rudeness, coldness, lack of interest, or selfishness as unimportant, or an accident. You may tell yourself, as I have, If this happens again, I will speak up. Of course it happens again, and you may or may not speak up. When you finally do find a bit of courage to speak your truth, the other party may be annoyed, dismissive, or, worse yet, accuse you of being too needy or controlling, or otherwise deflect responsibility. Usually the end result is that your love dismisses your concerns and feelings. As a result, to be in a relationship you may retreat into compliance and minimize your own relational needs. Because the resulting feelings of disappointment may be too overwhelming to face, you may bargain with yourself by focusing on that person's positive attributes. I say to you lovingly, stop doing this to yourself. When you encounter this relationship dynamic it indicates that you may be trying too hard to be seen, heard, and loved.

A lot of us are potential junkies, especially if we are a highly sensitive person (HSP), or an empath, as I am. We have the beautiful ability to see people not as they present themselves in the moment, but as they would be in their most actualized, ideal potential. We may begin to hope that if we continue to see and treat people as if they are living as their best selves, they will then evolve into the best version of themselves . . . and then be able to love us as we desire to be loved.

I have seen this method fail time and time again. We then end up picking up the pieces of our beautiful self, offered to someone who wasn't able to value us in the way we deserve.

As you read this, perhaps you are reflecting on a time when you experienced this kind of disappointment or loss in a relationship. Or you may be in that place now.

I have good news. We can heal this core wound by way of personal independence within ourselves. We can learn the inestimable value of our own worth and draw in a wonderful partner as a result. We are priceless beings who deserve to be honored for all that we are and all that we are not. We don't have to be perfect to be loved. It is through being vulnerable, uncertain, and honest that we progressively reveal our authentic selves.

You may consider prioritizing meditation, prayer, self-development, and healing in order to shift the pattern of giving your power away to a partner or a potential partner. It may feel difficult initially to release painful memories of times that you compromised your value and worth. You may enlist the help of a holistic healing practitioner, a life coach, or a psychotherapist to assist you in the process, yet it will be invaluable to take these steps and invest in yourself.

I encourage you to give yourself a solid chunk of time to work on loving the person that you are right now. Give yourself time to go to the depths of how you can gift yourself with your own authentic presence, and with the power of your own loving kindness. I am here to assist you, should you want to reach out.

As you begin to put your emotional health and well-being first, you will find that you will develop increased knowledge of what makes you happy *and* what doesn't make you happy. You will know where and with whom you *do* resonate, and where and with whom you *do not.*

You will learn to honor and listen to your own inner voice. Eventually others will follow your lead and begin to treat you with increasing kindness, understanding, empathy, and respect. This unfolding and simultaneous mirroring is a transformational experience.

Friendships and romantic love can then be created from fully knowing and valuing your own unique identity, preferences, abilities, and needs. From the outset, from within, you will affirm your true self as being complete and whole. From this more self-articulated and confident place you will be able to attract relationships that accurately mirror and complement you.

I have found it important to develop self-nurturing routines that consist of an array of activities I can enjoy with or without someone else. I also began to talk to myself with encouragement. For instance, every day I tell myself, "I love you." I suggest that you define activities to do alone and with others. Wake up each morning and say to yourself out loud, "I love you."

To create avenues for self-expression and pleasure, I suggest you develop interests, be they in the arts, music, sports, writing; having a pet; sexually pleasing yourself; or through stage performance. Exploring activities for fun—such as hiking, swimming, biking, rock climbing, dancing, karaoke, skiing, and walking—are also healthy ways to expand. Doing some of these activities alone and some within a group setting can strengthen your unique sense of self and identity.

The shadow side of Chiron in Libra may be hidden in your unconscious and manifest in patterns that trigger the unwanted criticism of you versus bringing about the desired understanding and empathy you wish to receive. Tendencies for those of you with Chiron in Libra would be the potential to lose your identity completely in a total merging with an intimate partner or with friends, associates, or family members. You may subjugate your own needs to serve those of others and then feel resentful.

People may criticize you because you act like a chameleon: If you perceive the environment to be emotionally unsafe for you, you change your opinion (or mind) in order to keep the peace, hide out, or fit in as protection from imagined (or real) criticism or perceived danger. Working to be your authentic self and also setting healthy boundaries with others when necessary will help you change this pattern of minimizing yourself to people please.

As you develop your inner resources to identify and express your preferences, without fear of being judged or rejected, you will progressively let go of the masks you have worn to conceal your genuine and beautiful heart, talents, and proclivities.

You may have retained childhood wounds that were a result of your being ridiculed, shamed, or abused, which can be best healed with loving support from trusted family members, friends, and healing professionals. The safety and trust found in these relationships will help you to reemerge as a more integrated version of yourself.

Ꭷ *Takeaways*

- Ꭷ Practice developing a loving and kind relationship with yourself by scheduling time to explore engaging in and enjoying various activities that you can do by yourself. For example, take a favorite book to a park or the beach, rent a movie, prepare a superb meal for yourself, schedule a massage, or receive a Reiki treatment. The purpose is to decorate your own soul and nurture yourself in caring ways.

꩜ Take a class to learn something you're curious about. Or attend a community event centered on a cause that's important to you. Join and attend an online Meetup group to make connections with new people who are like-minded. In these ways you begin to define and articulate what you enjoy.

꩜ Forge sensual connections with yourself by listening to music, lighting a candle and taking a bubble bath, or going on a walk in nature or downtown. Be sexual with yourself, and learn your own body so that you will be able to fully surrender to a blissful experience with a partner. Be able to express what you do and do not enjoy, without apology.

꩜ *Affirmations*

"I know myself and love myself."
"I trust my inner voice."
"Sharing my preferences makes me happy."
"I create my own happiness."
"I express my sexuality fully without shame."

13
Chiron in Scorpio

Core Wounding in the Experience and Expression of Power

Wounded Chiron Feels

Paranoid

Insensitive

Addicted to sex

Unable to manage anger

Healed Chiron Feels

Trusting

Sensitive

A sense of belonging

Emotionally intuitive

Let's begin this chapter with a few historical events that took place when Chiron was in Scorpio, which exemplify the essence of this placement's core wounding. It centers on power and its use—both aligned power and abusive power. In 1947, in a healthy use of presidential power, U.S. President Harry Truman signed the National Security Act into law and established the Department of Defense, the Joint Chiefs of Staff, and the National Security Council.

In what still causes feelings of grief and murmurings of foul play, under Chiron in Scorpio, Princess Diana tragically died in 1997. Demonstrating the abuse of power, one of the largest mass suicides in U.S. history was orchestrated by Heaven's Gate, an American UFO religious cult based near San Diego, California. In 1997 thirty-nine members were found dead, misled to believe that they were ascending to the "evolutionary level above human" by their leaders, Marshall Applewhite and Bonnie Nettles. What significance and information does Chiron in Scorpio hold for you?

The sign of Scorpio is all about power, other people's resources, animal instincts, sexuality, and persuasiveness. Your psychoastrology with Chiron in the sign of Scorpio is centered on your experience and expression of power on a spectrum. This means that you may fear your power, or conversely abuse your power. Another way to look at this: Most likely you have experienced a misalignment and misuse of power. For instance, you may employ self-sabotage and hurt yourself or, conversely, abuse others. You may experience a deep fear and mistrust of others that is very hard to alleviate. A core dilemma for you is wondering how to manage these difficult feelings of mistrust that you feel in your body. Your emotions may ride the full spectrum, up to and including paranoia.

To avoid feeling the vulnerable emotions of pain and fear triggered by mistrust, you self-protectively hide your sensitive heart. Underneath the complex vetting methods you employ in determining if someone is worthy of your trust is an ever-present fear of annihilation and death. This is painful for you because you enjoy deeply intense emotional and physical connections with others. The key to healing this pattern is in progressively trusting your ability to be vulnerable *and* feel safe.

With Chiron in Scorpio you may have an innate ability to connect with deeper truths on topics related to philosophy, religion, metaphysics, astrology, psychology, life, death, love, and loss. Many metaphysical traditions teach that the death you fear is not to your physical body, but to your ego or false self. The ego is the part of us that may pose as self-love. Yet in its drive to protect us from potential hurt and loss, it may sabotage us by pushing others away, thus causing the loss we fear. Again, in this instance, our ego informs us of potential danger, but it may actually be our self-hatred in disguise. Believing we are protecting ourselves, our unhealed fear and pain causes us to distance or separate ourselves, even decidedly reject others. Those of us with Chiron in Scorpio actually can, in this way, create a sense of loneliness and disconnection.

The psychoastrology of Chiron in Scorpio facilitates your ego mind to find fault with yourself and blame others for your perceived status in life. You are especially hard on yourself and may pepper yourself with critical thoughts and judgments. As a natural outgrowth of that thinking, blame and criticism bleeds out onto others whom you are close to.

Instead of wounding yourself and others from this outdated operating system of self-sabotage, let's look to possible solutions. We can choose instead to lean into our judgments, criticisms, and fears, to ask them what information they contain. Often your heart wants you to connect with and listen to these deep longings.

You have a powerful intuitive ability and sensitivity that is usually stronger than that of your peers and your family. Your intuitive gifts and your healing abilities shine forth when you connect to your deep inner wisdom. Your innate gifts also grow as you increasingly expose your inner self to others. You thereby embrace the fear of being overwhelmed by close connections with others. This shared vulnerability is what builds trust in relationships.

Yes, opening your generous heart to another person could very well hurt you. You risk being betrayed, disappointed, or abandoned. However, your heart has the potential to break open more fully with each experience of connection. Your heart grows in depth and breadth with every separation; and it heals each time if you guide it to. It's natural to be fearful and anxious as you progressively embrace a heart-centered place from which to live versus a cerebral-centered head space from which to live. As you make this transition, you simultaneously gain the capacity to contain and experience more unconditional love than you ever could before.

An issue for you to explore is the dynamic of comparing yourself to others. It might be clear that this process of self-judgment isn't working anymore. This thought pattern may stem from your having grown up in a household where your perceived shortcomings were held over your head and used as examples of your "many failures."

With Chiron in Scorpio, you may have adopted negative beliefs about yourself. This is termed an *introject* in the psychotherapy community. To clarify, an introject is defined as a false belief about ourselves that has been handed down to us by another person of influence, usually a primary caretaker or family system. This belief we embrace as truth and then make it a part of our self-concept.

When you learn to stop judging yourself to be less than who you are, and let go of comparing yourself to others, the healing process can truly begin. This type of inner self-abuse through criticism obstructs the truth of who you really are. You are a powerful being who was called to Earth as an expression of love; you have the ability to become a transformational leader.

Comparing yourself to others is a thought habit you can choose to extinguish now in this moment. When you are engaged in a cycle of self-judgment, your central nervous system is in a constant state of activation and high alert. In your waking life, this constant state of hyperalertness and hypervigilance means you are on guard 100 percent of the time. You may appear edgy, anxious, agitated, and critical and are challenging to be around. As a result, people may misperceive you as being hardened or insensitive, which is far from the truth of who you really are! You are very sensitive, perceptive, and intuitive.

You might benefit greatly from engagement in a meditation practice, either in a group setting or on your own. Practices that settle your central nervous system back to a baseline of peace and nonactivation will be transformative in a positive sense for you.

Association with a community involving the exploration of topics that are centered on various uses and abuses of power can be found through engagement with the fields of philosophy, metaphysics, the Kabbalah, astrology, psychology, and spirituality (for example). Finding a resonance with like-minded individuals in these or other communities and traditions will facilitate your inner alignment.

You have the potential to use your capacities for the reformation of our planet, and that starts with your evolution as an individual. In this evolved state, you become magnetic to others, and this draws large numbers of people toward you. Many will want to hear your thoughts. Many will want to hear how you have learned to forgive yourself and that you now derive your strength from a sense of empathy and unconditional love. You have the ability to bring people together and deliver powerful, self-healing messages to them.

Do you find yourself shuddering at my suggestion of unconditional love and self-empathy as a healing balm? Opening yourself to the process of trusting someone may feel terrifying to you at this moment, but you can expand your capacity and heal the psychoastrology of Chiron by co-creating intimacy through gradual, mannered trust.

Unconditional love looks beyond our faults and flaws to our inherent perfection, which is the truth of who we all are at our sacred core. Life experiences, traumas, wounds, and abuse have caused many of us to shrink and move away from forming trusting relationships with others.

You may be afraid of loving deeply because you believe the person will leave you for some reason or other and, of course, will eventually die. This fear of losing the object of your love could be overwhelming for you, and challenging to resolve. If you are able to make the paradigm shifts necessary to embrace spirituality in a tradition that resonates with you, and integrate beliefs that support you, you will begin to assuage your fears.

As a healing practitioner and co-creator I embrace the belief that love never dies. Love changes form, but the essence and energy of a person, pet, or memory is with us forever, and eternally. This perspective is expressed in many traditions. A passage in *A Course in Miracles* reads as follows: "Nothing real can be threatened. Nothing unreal exists. Herein lies the peace of God."

What is peace for you? How can you expand on the sentiment that only love is real? How can you turn unconditional love toward yourself? How can you forgive yourself for all the recriminations that you hold against yourself?

You can be cruel to yourself with your thoughts, and that's not serving you anymore. It's time to adopt new ways of thinking and believing. You'd be well served to break with your past and to eventually find acceptance of the person you were then.

The transformative aspects of Chiron in Scorpio point to your ability to reframe life experiences into something of meaning. Through your own ability to deeply empathize with the intense, shared emotional experiences of others, you have an inherent ability to help others understand loss, grief, and death. There lives within you an innate intuitive ability to understand the deep mysteries of life, loss, and love.

There is healing available for you to heal from abuses of power that were experienced in your formative years, whether that was experienced in your family of origin or by peers. Learning to nurture the little one within you by attending to his, her, or their emotional, physical, and psychological needs will break the cycle of abusive power. Sharing your life story will help you and others to heal because in the mutuality of the dialogue you will develop trust. This shared vulnerability heals your psychoastrology. Writing a blog, starting a podcast, writing a book, sharing at a twelve-step program, or other similar pursuits empower you to change and deepen your relationship with your authentic self.

The shadow side of Chiron in Scorpio may be in your unconscious and manifest in behaviors and patterns that trigger the unwanted criticism of others, instead of bringing about the desired understanding you wish to receive from them. A negative behavioral pattern to watch for would be the potential to seek revenge when you've been hurt. If left untreated, your shadow self can be prone to dark, jealous, and potentially violent impulses. The powerlessness you feel fuels the propensity to hurt others as well as yourself. You may damage yourself or a loved one with thoughts, words, or actions.

Also watch out for the tendency to use your sexuality to gain power. Sexuality can be immensely healing and, conversely, destructive. Sex can provide a false sense of closeness that may be devoid of love entirely. Experiencing your sexuality as a vehicle for powerful transformation can be both wounding and healing. Address your impulses to inflict wounding with your sexuality or sexual addiction. When necessary, seek treatment with a healing practitioner or sex therapist to aid you. The container of the sacred therapeutic space creates a safe place for you to more deeply explore these issues.

Plugging into spirituality or a formalized meditation practice centered in compassion can help you work through the powerful undercurrents that tempt you to act out the impulses of the shadow self. Developing a sense of belonging is key for you to heal the core wounds and psychoastrology of Chiron in Scorpio. Being part of something larger than yourself feeds the longing in your soul for emotional connection. As well, it quenches the thirst for closeness.

Forming a close relationship with someone you admire (perhaps a teacher, mentor, parent, sibling, guru, professor, or guide) can help you develop alternative coping skills to help you process your feelings of pain, anger, helplessness, or rage. Seek professional assistance if you have thoughts of harming yourself or others.

ꜟ *Takeaways*

- ꜟ You enjoy being generous, so look for opportunities to volunteer and assist with a disenfranchised population that you value. You will notice feeling connected to your inner reservoir of potential when you give back in ways that are meaningful to you. Some examples include volunteering to feed the homeless population in your area, at an animal shelter or rescue, to become a Big Brother/Big Sister, or a Court Appointed Special Advocates (CASA) volunteer for abused and neglected children in the court system, or maybe even adopting a pet.

- ꜟ Try a ropes course, a climbing or rappelling class with a partner, or other team-building courses that is best done with a partner. Explore ways to work on issues of vulnerability and trust in safe and professional environments.

- ꜟ Come up with self-starter projects and pinpoint specific people to ask to help you. In this way you are practicing both asking for help and experiencing the receiving of it, all of which builds trust. You are developing the use of your power by exercising the muscle of interdependence, which promotes the construct of shared needs being mutually met.

- ꜟ Explore opportunities with hospice, nursing homes, and other long-term care facilities to assist people who are dealing with the dying. You have an innate gift in your ability to bridge the immaterial and metaphysical world with the material and earthly world.

ꜟ *Affirmations*

"I use my power for goodness."
"I am learning to trust."
"I am safe."
"Everything is always working out for me."
"I am generous and kind."

14

Chiron in Sagittarius

Core Wounding in Truth and Illusion

Wounded Chiron Feels
Self-righteous
Argumentative
Blunt

Healed Chiron Feels
Committed to justice
Adventurous
Self-empowered

The psychoastrology illuminated by Chiron in Sagittarius is centered on illusion being presented as the truth, which is also known as deception. Healing your core wounding is found by bringing injustices to light and holding offenders accountable. Restitution may be sought through the proper channels—be they legal or legislatively based—and by establishing alliances and treaties where appropriate for safeguarding. The NATO Alliance signed in 1949 under Chiron in Sagittarius is an example of one such treaty enacted to unify and strengthen the military response of the Western Allies to a possible invasion of Western Europe by the Soviet Union and its Warsaw Pact allies. In 2001, the towers of the World Trade Center and the Pentagon were bombed on September 11, and George W. Bush subsequently declared a Global War on Terrorism to launch an ongoing effort to thwart terrorists before they acted, as an attempt to safeguard the United States.

A historic event highlighting the core wounding of illusion being presented as truth occurred in the 1950s in the McCarthy era. Senator Joseph McCarthy and his followers conducted illegal trials using unsubstantiated accusations of subversion or treason. These practices ruined countless lives and careers, their goal being to highlight and dramatize the inflammatory Red Scare. Let's take a personal look at what Chiron in Sagittarius means for you.

If your Chiron is in the sign of Sagittarius, the core wounding you have experienced has affected your ability to differentiate between what is true and what may be false. You may conceptualize this inner dilemma by having difficulty in developing a solid belief system or in accessing a higher self that accurately ascertains the truth. Either way, you feel you are not able to perceive yourself, your life, or the world around you clearly.

By having to adapt from an early age to an invalidating environment, your upbringing has left you with a sense of self-disempowerment. There was illusion and hypocrisy surrounding you, and you wondered why no one was doing anything about it. As a child or teenager you didn't have the power to do anything yourself; therefore, you may have had no recourse other than to bottle up your anger, rage, or sadness. You needed more support to find your own truth and develop your belief systems. Now is the time to address your beliefs and stand strong in what you believe to be true!

You are idealistic, in the best sense of that word. You value high morality, and enjoy doing what is right for the greater good.

At the same time, you may experience a disruption in feeling connected to something greater than yourself, higher truths, and your spirituality. You may not yet know how to connect with the vastness beyond yourself.

You may find this connection in secular or religious/spiritual pursuits. Other areas or endeavors to explore include those found in the world of nature; reading, taking a long walk; meditating or praying; attending church, a synagogue, or the mosque; joining a spiritual community or engaging in Bible study; familiarizing yourself with metaphysics, the Kabbalah, philosophy, astrology, or Eastern philosophy; or by being of service to others as a volunteer, as a peer leader, or through political activism.

There is no limit to what you can explore in order to find personal meaning and belief. The gift comes when you are able to look at your life as an adventure and find belonging within the context of larger purpose.

Areas you may resonate with are higher education and learning, foreign travel, politics, and the legal field. As you have natural proclivities in these areas of interest, you should consider exploring them to find meaning in your new life.

On your journey to wholeness, it can help you to view your experiences through the lens of curiosity, and find ways to derive pleasure from investigating new practices that will bring you comfort and inner peace and help you answer the question, Why am I here?

Examples of how Chiron in Sagittarius brings what is hidden from the shadows into the light include the #MeToo movement, the subsequent Time Person of the Year 2017 being the "silence breakers" (those who brought this movement to the forefront by revealing the sexual assault and harassment they experienced), and the continuing news and social media coverage of the movement and public exposure of men in power who have abused women. This is exactly how Chiron in Sagittarius brings what is hidden in the shadows into the light.

Hollywood has denounced male leaders who have harassed, abused, and assaulted women. Our country is divided over the presidency of Donald Trump. Some think Trump is making America great again; some think he is the face of what is wrong with our country.

Issues around sexual harassment in the workplace have given rise to employers conducting sensitivity trainings and adopting a zero-tolerance policy for these crimes. We are seeing the personal become political. Women in particular are rising up to take their place at the political table.

If you are a woman, I encourage you to speak up for your rights as a woman. If you are a male reader, I applaud those of you who are standing up for us and supporting us. If you are transgender, I bow to your courage for openly being who you are in the public sphere, thereby forcing lawmakers to validate your equal rights to life, liberty, and the pursuit of happiness.

I believe that what will help America to heal is naturally found in the full potential of Chiron in Sagittarius. Chiron in this sign inspires creative legislative change, which impacts generations of people to come. This same change will inspire the implementation of legislation to keep guns out of the hands of children and adolescents, terrorists, gang members, convicted criminals, and persons who are mentally ill. The same force will aid us to provide our veterans (who, after all, fought to protect our rights) with the supportive services they need. Health care reform and providing a way for immigrants to stay and work in our country speaks to the same revolution. If some of these causes are important to you, taking action is a way for you to heal the psychoastrology of your Chiron in Sagittarius.

Those of you with Chiron in Sagittarius may find aspects of Chiron's core wounding buried so deeply in your unconscious and so out of your awareness that your behaviors may incur the unwanted criticism of others, instead of what you really desire: understanding and empathy. Behaviors for you to watch out for include a tendency to be blunt, so much so that the feelings of others may be hurt. You may value being *right* over being *loved or loving*. This may mean that you are perceived as self-righteous, or even argumentative. One unfortunate result of this behavior pattern is that you push others away instead of drawing them in to share your ideas and beliefs. You can achieve inner peace when you learn that you don't have to be "right" to be grounded in your truth. Allowing others to find their own way will be liberating for you.

Extending forgiveness and empathy to yourself can help you soften your judgments of yourself; you may then be able to deliver messages of truth *with love* to others. Remember, finding your personal mission statement will be healing for you, and studying spiritual truths can help you to enhance and strengthen your own belief system.

✑ Takeaways

- Develop a sense of connection to as many things of interest as you can think of. Explore them by becoming involved with people, places, and things that offer engagement with those interests.

- Google topics related to "finding meaning and purpose" and see what comes up that intrigues you! I found over twenty-nine million in my own search. Notice books you might read, videos you might watch, and podcasts to listen to. Or start your own blog or podcast, or write articles and submit them for publication.

- TED and TEDx are platforms for inspirational people to share their ideas and philosophies and to expand our minds. Check some of them out to see how you may be inspired to take action. Apply to give a TED or TEDx Talk!

- Consider auditing a class, just to learn for learning's sake. Go on a vision quest, an ayahuasca retreat, or a yoga/meditation retreat, for instance. Explore similar practices and experiences that resonate with you.

ꙅ *Affirmations*

"I am connected to my higher self."

"My core beliefs support me."

"I find deep meaning and connection to life."

"I am truth."

"I have inner clarity."

15

Chiron in Capricorn

*Core Wounding in Responsibility,
Achievement, and Success*

Wounded Chiron Feels

Controlling

Greedy

A fear of failing

Opportunistic

Healed Chiron Feels

Mindful

Able to ask for help

Confident

Able to set boundaries

et's begin with a look at historical events influenced by Chiron in Capricorn. Healing the psychoastrology of our core wounding caused by greed, excessive control, restriction, or usury is found by setting boundaries and developing healthy self-esteem. We saw this take place back in the 1950s as our ever-increasing debt-laden society initiated the Diner's Club credit card, thereby promoting the "buy now, pay later" economic culture that represents both the positive and negative potential of Chiron in Capricorn. In 2004, the dedication of the World War II Memorial took place in Washington, D.C., as a way to commemorate the achievement of the more than four hundred thousand Americans who gave their lives in World War II. When healed and aligned, Chiron in Capricorn gives credit where credit is due. So what does Chiron in Capricorn mean for your psychoastrology?

As you grew up as a child, your core wounding occurred through the hurtful ways that you were criticized for not being good enough or successful enough. This wounding experience was internalized into your self-concept as the not-good-enough inner child. Your adult self may still be carrying the experience around as a body memory, with the associated limiting belief of "I am not good enough."

You may often be unconscious of this part of yourself until a wound is triggered. As a result, you may actively avoid being criticized because the result may be a flood of powerful negative emotions. These derive from your inner child who was shamed for not meeting unrealistic expectations, or conversely was not praised for the wonderful age-appropriate tasks you *did* master.

These early memory impressions are awake today in the core wounds that point to your sense of achievement, responsibility, and success. As a result, you may be overly controlling and restrictive, or conversely, overly willing to give control to others.

With Chiron in Capricorn, you may experience a compulsive need to succeed, yet at the same time feel like you are never quite enough, or truly adequate, or sincerely gratified. This experience is destabilizing for you because you are, in fact, perceived to be successful, and you put forth great effort in the name of achievement. You really want to make a difference through your chosen endeavors.

When you fear you will fail, or become impatient with the process of reaching a goal, you may compromise ethics for personal gain and in the name of greed. This could manifest as telling a white lie every now and then to boost the appearance of, say, numbers. The compensatory behaviors of usury and deceit are present to guard against feelings of inadequacy. This tendency for deception is something to be on the lookout for and then to correct.

The compensatory behaviors of usury and deceit are present to guard against feelings of inadequacy. Whether or not you have been acknowledged for your true merit, or conversely manipulated circumstances to attain merit, you are often perceived as successful and, as such, may expend energy to keep your positive image up. This can be draining for you to maintain.

A better use of your energy and resources would be to ask for guidance or help from colleagues and mentors in the areas of organization, planning, and scheduling. Because you are a capable and self-reflective person you often need just a little bit of suggestion or guidance to change. You will experience emotional freedom as you ask for help and allow others to assist you. As a result of your own healing and newly gained confidence, you may choose to become a mentor to others.

The use of positive affirmations, such as, "I can do this," "I *am* enough," and "I am doing the best I can today with what I know," will help you learn to trust that the progressive steps you invest in reaching a goal will bring you the recognition, praise, and positive reputation that is so important to your healthy self-esteem.

In reaching for a goal, we often need to establish the boundaries required to accomplish it. Proficiency in setting these healthy boundaries is important for you to master. The negotiation of your needs and their parameters are areas for you to focus your decisions on each day. Take the appropriate time-out, and discuss uncertainties with a trusted friend or colleague.

We typically make decisions and negotiations unconsciously

throughout our day without much thought given to their potentially positive or negative consequences. Bringing presence and consciousness to the moment, from a mindfulness perspective, will help you establish and maintain balance in your personal and professional life. You will then be able to flow from a place of authenticity, allowing you to succeed and affording you the respect of others.

If your core wounding goes unacknowledged and is ignored by you, you are criticized rather than supported by others. In short, the shadow side of Chiron in Capricorn may be hidden in your unconscious and manifest in behaviors that trigger the painful judgments of others, instead of bringing about the desired understanding and empathy you wish to receive.

These issues for you to be mindful of are found in the areas of your life related to success, usury, and prestige. Watch for the potential tendencies to engage in activities and behaviors that result in your being perceived as a shrewd opportunist or, worst of all, as a user. You enjoy success, and when that impulse goes unchecked you may go on a power trip and put gains ahead of people and their feelings. In the movie *The Wolf of Wall Street,* Leonardo DiCaprio's character is the epitome of Chiron in Capricorn's shadow self. He was ruthless in achieving financial power and success without regard for how his behaviors negatively affected those around him.

Identifying ways to be productively of service to others is a way to heal areas of vulnerability and weakness. Look for win/win opportunities, and manifest them when starting a business. Start a charity, volunteer organization, or community development group. These are just a few examples of how you can use your skills in an exemplary way.

ɞ *Takeaways*

- ⚕ Offer to help someone else succeed in the accomplishment of his or her own goal setting with measurable and observable markers that you establish together to determine your progress. Often by helping someone else, you find fulfillment and healing for your own soul. This act of reparenting your inner child allows for self-acceptance and forgiveness for the parts of yourself you may have repressed and judged.

§ Do something once a week for the pure joy of it! This might be going for an ice cream or taking a walk in a park or on the beach. Other examples of relaxation and enjoyment could be going to a movie, reading a book for pleasure, going to a concert, experiencing sexual satisfaction, or buying flowers for yourself.

§ Find a teacher, mentor, trainer, coach, class, or support group, and ask for help in an area that you struggle with or find to be underdeveloped. No one can do everything, so allow your learning process to be fun. Accept that growth, mistakes, and imperfections are par for the course. They will occur as part of your learning curve; this is a natural and normal part of developing new skills. Find humor in your mishaps. Learn to laugh at yourself instead of hiding your mistakes or judging yourself for having made them.

∂ *Affirmations*

"I am good enough just as I am."
"I will reach my goals."
"I ask for help when I need it."
"I radiate success."
"People can depend on me."

16

Chiron in Aquarius

··

Core Wounding in Connection and Community

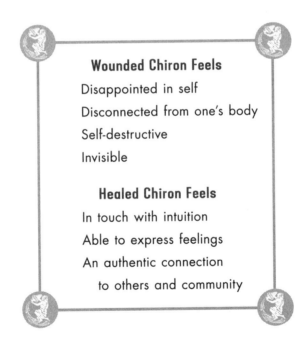

Wounded Chiron Feels

Disappointed in self

Disconnected from one's body

Self-destructive

Invisible

Healed Chiron Feels

In touch with intuition

Able to express feelings

An authentic connection

to others and community

Fidel Castro came to power in Cuba in 1959 under the influence of Chiron in Aquarius, exemplifying this placement's core wounding with the theme of disconnection from community. Castro wounded the Cuban people by isolating and disconnecting them from the rest of the world through Communism. Chiron in Aquarius's healing is found through verbal expression. In 2005 Hurricane Katrina brought devastation *and* the coming together of the world community in support. This one natural disaster represents both the wounding of Chiron in Aquarius through the destruction of a community and at the same time the healing of Chiron in Aquarius through the rebuilding of community, specifically New Orleans and the Gulf Coast. In 2008, after three decades, Bill Gates officially left his full-time position at Microsoft to concentrate on the Bill & Melinda Gates Foundation, representing a beautiful aspect of healed Chiron in Aquarius through service to the community at large. What does it mean for you to have Chiron in Aquarius?

Those of us with Chiron in the sign of Aquarius experience our core wounding in the area of our ability or inability to connect with others to create community. If you have Chiron in Aquarius, the difficulty you have connecting with, and then actually belonging to, a community can create a profound feeling of disconnection and isolation, even when you are physically part of a group. This experience is compounded by the fact that you have a hard time connecting to your own body, and with physical environments in general.

In other words, you have a hard time feeling that you fit in. This translates to a sense of disconnection and unbalance in your interpersonal life. You do not have a connection to an innate sense of knowing that you are important and loved. This is a painful place to be. You experience an unceasing feeling of having never found—or having lost—your tribe; thus, you may feel as if you live as a nomad in a foreign land. At the same time, you may be employed in a profession that requires you to build community with those you work with.

You may reexperience these feelings of core wounding if you relocate by moving to a new city. You may feel a sense of being alone even though you are surrounded by millions of people in a large metropolitan area. You may wonder if you will ever find where you fit in.

You may spend your first couple of years using navigation apps to figure out how to get from point A to point B; for example, from home to work, or to the grocery store, favorite restaurants, the gym, or church. It might help you when you feel displaced or suffer pangs of loneliness to recall to mind *why* you made this move in the first place, and what exactly would you like to create in your new environment in terms of your own unique community. By consistently investing yourself in your new location, you will cross a tipping point, and know within yourself that you are making progress in creating a community for yourself. This will feel inwardly nurturing to you.

Tapping back into your motivation for making the change and finding purpose in your new home can reconnect you to a deeper sense of meaning, which can be self-soothing and calming during moments of emotional upset. Your new geographic location can become a secure base for you over time. It can help to remind you that you are creating stability each and every day. This can bring a sense of newfound accomplishment to your life.

If you maintain spiritual practices or grounding belief systems, incorporate them into the creation of your community. Ask for spiritual guidance, and for signs to be shown to you regarding where and with whom you fit in and resonate with. We are powerful creators and may lose sight of that when feeling these core wounds of disconnection and isolation. Remind yourself that change is constantly occurring, even when you cannot see it. Wheels are in motion on your behalf that you do not know about. And if these words do not resonate with you, then create a narrative you believe in and can hold on to for comfort.

Begin to notice what happens around you as a result. Be present as you pass people in the street and you go about your daily business. Your encounters with others may take on more significance as a result of being mindfully present. Try to create relationships with new people, some of which will stick, others not so much. Some personal interactions may include having a meaningful conversation with someone you'd like to get to know better or sharing a moment or a meal with someone else and then parting ways.

Cultivating present-moment awareness can shift your core wounding experience of disconnection. What can you do to get started in finding new ways to connect with others? What is it that brings meaning and purpose to your life? How can you begin to feel into that creative space during the personal interactions that will begin to unfold for you? After I moved part-time from New Orleans to Los Angeles, I employed the mindfulness methods that I am offering you in order to grow my new community. When speaking with people who came along my path, I did my best to focus my attention on the present moment. Whether they were the Lyft or Uber driver, a cashier, the parking attendant, or a person next to me in line at the grocery store, I gave each conversation my full attention. I also asked people how they were and paused to listen for their answer. This changed my life for the better. Today I still remind myself throughout the day to try to be fully present when listening to others, and to not lapse into forgetfulness and hurry.

So that you're not in a rush, a possible solution to allow more relaxed time into your day would include leaving the house a bit earlier for your destination or appointment. This sets you up so that you may relax into and enjoy the moments that unfold before you. This practice has resulted in unexpected, positive conversations and encounters for me wherein I had plenty of time to pause and engage. I wonder if you might consider these or other techniques to practice in your own life so that you, too, can be available for a greater connection with others.

I found it helpful to refresh my intention each day so that I would remember to actively listen to the people I might encounter on my path. It was easy to forget and fall back into the old pattern of rushing to my next appointment or event. I was patient with myself.

I am grateful to be able to share this with you because I do believe that it will help you to develop a community that will be significant to you. Allow yourself the gift of slowing down just a little bit in order to be open to those individuals who have been placed in your path. You may even be the gift that they need today.

All that said, the isolation and social anxiety you experience may lead you to avoid reaching out to others and forming the close personal relationships you desire. Whenever I feel anxious in a conversation I try to inwardly acknowledge that anxiety to myself, and then shift my focus back to the words being spoken to me by the person right in front of me.

By using this practice of shifting from *me* to *them,* with repetition and over time, eventually my feelings of anxiety are assuaged. If I have nothing to say, I've learned to just listen and excuse myself when I want to end the conversation. It's my wish to be able to communicate in a genuine way that resonates with me, and not just fill silence or be "polite." You may want to try these techniques, or create new ones, and see if your anxiety begins to dissipate and subside as a result.

Even the most socially adept individuals may have had to learn to manage their social anxiety to one degree or another. I have had to myself, and I learned that when faced with my own fears of being judged or criticized by others, I have decided to name my fears and face them, instead of allowing them to paralyze me and prevent me from attending an event or going to a party. Fear is the emotion that underlies social anxiety, and it wants to isolate you and prevent you from having meaningful connections. After all, experience has told you that it's always been safer that way. However, be assured that, if your Chiron is in the sign of Aquarius, the healing you need is found through connection with others, while learning to manage any concurrent anxiety.

The fears we have are often unrealistic, especially in regard to thoughts and beliefs we may struggle with when considering whether or not to attend a social event. Do any of these statements sound familiar: "Will I know anyone there?" "What if 'so and so' is there?" "What if 'so and so' is *not* there?" "I'm not good in big groups." "I don't know what to talk about." "I'm too fat to be seen." "I don't know why 'so and so' dislikes me, and they will probably be there." "I dislike these 'superficial' parties where no one talks about anything of meaning and value."

These are all self-deprecating thoughts, disguised as excuses to keep us separate from the potential experience of connecting with others. When making a shift in this area, what I offer for you to consider is the next time you are invited to a social event, decide to view it as holding the pure potential for connection and community building.

You may make it a point to say hello to everyone in attendance and ask how they're doing, and then truly listen with empathy and openness to their answers. You may decide to speak with a select few who resonate with you and find out, in detail, how their lives are actually going, and then share, in an authentic way, how things are going for you. You may decide to attend the event for a set amount of time that feels good, and then leave before you become depleted or feel overwhelmed.

Even the most socially adept individuals may have had to learn to manage their social anxiety to one degree or another. I have had to myself, and I learned that when faced with my own fears of being judged or criticized by others, I have decided to name my fears and face them instead of allowing them to paralyze me and prevent me from attending an event or going to a party.

In any given social or professional event we each have the opportunity to engage at the level of comfort that works for us. Learn what it is you need to feel comfortable and authentically connected and energized. Respect your boundaries, and listen to both your inner voice and your body's natural intelligence; they will guide you. It's also very helpful to maintain a connection to your sources of inspiration.

The healing of your psychoastrology comes through your search to become a part of a cause that is larger than yourself; it is also found through meaningful connection with others. Get creative with this process, and make it fun! Finding healthy connections with others may be more fun to pursue if shared in the context of a humanitarian cause that you care about.

This pairing together of a meaningful cause with personal interactions brings you pleasure and a sense of fulfilled purpose. Associating in ways that bring meaning and enjoyment to your life are gateways to healing the former sense of isolation that's found in the core wounding of Aquarius. In this way your mind and heart begin to integrate as one.

The shadow side of Chiron in Aquarius may be hidden in your unconscious and can manifest in behaviors we engage in that could trigger the painful judgments of others, instead of bringing about the desired outcomes and empathy that you wish to receive. Be aware of times when your need for isolation excludes other people, for you may inadvertently push people away. This can become a scenario of self-sabotage when you privately desire closeness but outwardly reject it from others. In this way you may appear to be emotionally cold and distant.

It can be helpful for you to monitor the avoidant type of attachment behavior. Thus, I suggest that you review the different attachment styles in the material that discusses that; it's found in chapter 4 beginning on page 61. It may also serve you to enter therapy (or a similar professional relationship) to explore any trauma or abuse you may have experienced that caused you to employ these defense mechanisms for protection. Sometimes we need a deep healing process that allows us to open up to love and connection with others. This is a natural part of your psychoastrological journey and process. Give yourself a safe place to express your emotions and explore your wounds so that they may be healed.

I'll leave you with this quote from Marianne Williamson: "We are taught to fear rather than to love one another. We perceive a world of scarcity—of lack, of danger—and from that perception we conclude that we must compete to get our needs met at the expense of whomever else. In truth, it is our perception of separation that creates the scarcity to begin with. . . . Fear is the power of our minds turned against ourselves—the loveless, dissociated, despairing self. It's our self-hatred posing as self-love."

Let's together commit to choosing self-love for ourselves so we can then share it with others and create meaningful connections in our world.

ᗭ *Takeaways*

- Set the intention to define experiences in which you find meaning. Begin the practice of using a written or audio journal in which to log your thoughts and feelings. Identify places and events of social connection with people where you may find a sense of belonging. Do this a minimum of once per month, and increase to weekly participation over time.

- Ask a like-minded person to go out to do something of shared interest. Examples include going out for coffee, a cocktail, a meal, a movie, or a musical event or going out in nature for a hike, a bike ride, or a walk. You might instead attend an art opening or a cooking class, or explore a humanitarian or volunteer opportunity. Sharing some of what is written in your journal may be a starting point for deeper dialogue and connection.

- Choose to confide in a trusted source about your feelings of isolation, and ask that person if they ever feel the same way. This is one way to begin to know that others may also be experiencing feelings of disconnection similar to your own. Making meaningful connection by opening up about your feelings can create new channels of connection that heal the core wounds of Chiron in Aquarius.

☙ Join a group or network centered on common topics of interest; for instance, a community gardening project, a twelve-step program, a Meetup group, or a book club.

☙ *Affirmations*

"I allow myself to experience connection."

"I step out of fear and into love."

"My contributions are significant."

"I am connected."

"I am loved."

17

Chiron in Pisces

Core Wounding in Self-Care and the Immaterial World

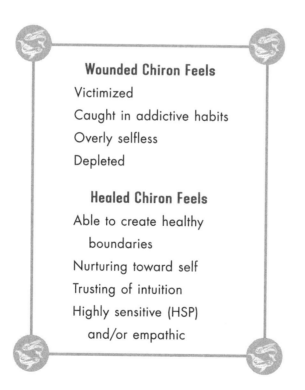

Wounded Chiron Feels

Victimized

Caught in addictive habits

Overly selfless

Depleted

Healed Chiron Feels

Able to create healthy
    boundaries

Nurturing toward self

Trusting of intuition

Highly sensitive (HSP)
    and/or empathic

So here you are; you have Chiron in the sign of Pisces. In the material world, your core wounds center on your struggle with self-care. In the immaterial world your core wounds were caused by early development experiences of victimization and betrayal. These wounds affect your ability to believe that there is fairness in the world, which you value. This disappointment has led you to feel intense loss and grief. You do not believe that there is a world that is truly safe for you to inhabit.

The 1960s, which you grew up in, was a unique time in American culture. The Beatles released *Sgt. Pepper's Lonely Hearts Club Band,* which was nicknamed the soundtrack of the Summer of Love. Where were the boundaries? How did you get the attention you needed? What was it like to be a "love" child? These are some of the issues you faced in creating an identity for yourself. Your needs may not have been adequately met.

You've compensated by an overdeveloped need to put others first. It may be hard for you to value yourself as highly as you prioritize others. This pattern, of course, inevitably leaves you feeling depleted; therefore, you have a propensity to turn to addictive habits for coping. Because you neglect your self-care, you may feel drained or exhausted. You may have favored helping others over helping yourself as a way to escape from your overwhelming and ever-increasing needs.

Because you give much of yourself to care for others, you experience confusion and frustration when you are mistakenly perceived and then judged as needy. I know how disappointing it feels when you are not appreciated for your efforts. As someone who has worked diligently to learn discernment about whom to serve and how and when to serve others, I'll share an example with you. I have learned that using my intuitive superpower is the surest and quickest way to lose my energy and life force. (This intuitive superpower thinks it knows what others need or want, and then, of course, it gives them what they have *not* asked for.)

Of course, I was left depleted. If you have found yourself in this or similar situations, I encourage you to take responsibility for it and enact the steps necessary to change on behalf of your own empowerment. Practice what it feels like to say "no" to people, places, and things that may deplete you. As is common when changing our behaviors, your pendulum may initially swing to the opposite extreme, and you may temporarily isolate yourself a bit as you search to find your balance.

Since you know that your tendency is to give too much, begin to practice the technique of allowing yourself to change your mind when necessary. I suggest that you enlist the partnership of a trusted person or two, and ask them if you can discuss and practice discerning personal boundaries with them, without criticism, blame, or shame. Once you have these accountability partners in place, begin to practice articulating healthy boundaries with them, which may feel liberating. It may also be anxiety producing since you are accustomed to people pleasing.

Let's face it; you are going to let some people down. And others may talk about you, but what they say might surprise you. When you make the decision to root deeply into your own value and self-worth, you may be surprised to find that your loved ones and peers respect you. Perhaps by your example you will permit them to anchor into *their* value and self-worth by being more authentic about their limitations also. You literally put old patterns and unhealthy dynamics out of the business of running your life.

The healing of your psychoastrology comes about by:

1. Learning to set healthy boundaries
2. Developing self-care practices that fill and maintain the reserves of your fuel tank
3. Through personal spirituality that nourishes your soul and spirit

Transformation comes when you confront, not escape, your existential crisis. It arrives when you turn *toward* the immaterial world. It manifests when you embrace, not fall *away* from, your intuitive gifts. This dualistic pattern shows us an aspect of the healing of the core wound of Chiron in Pisces. You have great natural intuitive abilities because you are sensitive, even possibly on the highly sensitive person

(HSP)/empath spectrum. You can learn more about being an empath from my friend and mentor Dr. Judith Orloff in her book *The Empath's Survival Guide: Life Strategies for Sensitive People.*

You have the potential to cultivate your abilities for powerful use in service to the greater good of humanity. Mother Teresa had Chiron in Pisces, and we know the changes she inspired on our planet during her lifetime and after her passing.

If you allow your shadow self to eclipse your good judgments, you may over time find yourself entrenched in addiction. The addictive habits may be a dependency on alcohol, drugs, sex, food, exercise, compulsive shopping, or hoarding, for instance.

Regardless of the behavior, self-criticism and self-judgment undermine your self-esteem. You can save yourself if you can ask for help. You can stop, shift, and change, one step at a time. If you commit to transformation you will find spiritual transcendence on the other side of the coin that we call addiction.

It might be the time in your life to enroll in metaphysically themed offerings by way of an intuitive development class, an online workshop, a certification program of study, or an in-depth immersion of spiritual study through a retreat experience.

Investing yourself in pursuits that take you outside of and beyond any addictive habits, patterns, and thoughts will aid in a natural letting go of any unhealthy need to escape. In its place you will cultivate joy and present-moment engagement with what has meaning and purpose for you. This connection will empower you, strengthen you, and open up your intuitive gifts.

In *Tears to Triumph: The Spiritual Journey from Suffering to Enlightenment*, author Marianne Williamson encapsulates your existential need to create meaning from life in order to fulfill your potential and find inner contentment: "Human existence is not just a random episode; with no higher purpose than that all of us should get what we want. Seen that way, with no overlay of service, spirit or connection;

our lives seem to lack ultimate meaning. The soul craves meaning the way the body craves oxygen. In the absence of a spiritual framework, we know the mechanics of life but stop short of understanding it. Failing to understand life, we misuse it. And misusing it, we cause suffering— for ourselves and for others."

Your healing comes when you learn to respect your own healthy limitations. Ask yourself, What is needed for me to heal? Allow space for the answers to come to you, and take the appropriate steps by enlisting others who can bear witness to your process. Engage in inner dialogue with your unresolved core wounding from betrayal and injustice by asking, What could the higher meaning be here for me, and then, how may I see this differently? Then listen to your own answers.

This practice of inner dialoguing with yourself cultivates your ability to lean in to your personal pain and ask what it has to tell you, or teach you, or warn you about. The inquiry not only gives you direction, it also facilitates a deeper connection to your intuition and spiritual guidance. You may want to try journaling to your higher power, God, the universe, Divine Mother, the Earth, or an ancestor, for instance, about an issue or problem that is causing you to feel stuck, and then write yourself a letter back, starting with "Dear _____." (Put your name in the blank.)

In finding connection to your higher consciousness there are many belief systems to draw on. Seemingly endless kinds of doctrines, ideologies, and courses of study whose platforms are secular, spiritual, religious, philosophical, humanitarian, or metaphysical exist.

By taking time to explore what resonates with positive valence (things that have intrinsic goodness), you will be able to determine what satisfies the craving you have to understand what lies beyond your finite human form. What you find meaning in can become the foundation of self-care strategies that align with your values.

Here is a visualization to use so that you won't forget the importance of your own self-care. I've borrowed it from the field of aviation. Surely you recall that prior to a plane's takeoff, the flight attendant makes the following announcement: "In case of a change in cabin pressure, an oxygen mask will drop from the overhead compartment. Please be sure to secure your own oxygen mask first, before assisting others with their masks."

The shadow side of Chiron in Pisces may be hidden in your unconscious, and manifest in actions and behaviors that result in painful judgments by others, instead of bringing about the desired understanding and empathy you wish to receive. Something for you to watch for specifically when you have been wounded by betrayal, or by an unjust victimization, is that you may push people, places, and things away through self-isolation. When you try to explain, justify, or defend yourself, you may be criticized as being a martyr, or you may be accused of acting from a "victim mentality."

As I discussed earlier, your propensity to give too much may leave you open to criticism. Watch for these self-sabotaging patterns and understand that you may tend to try to escape by losing yourself and your identity in any way, including by an addiction to alcohol, drugs, sex, shopping, food, self-criticism, people, exercise, places, things, or any other compulsions that may lead you away from embracing your beautiful and generous core self.

ꝋ Takeaways

- Identify what you need to forgive yourself for by making a list of experiences that still hurt you emotionally. Begin with the first memory that comes to mind, and perform this healing ritual: Place one of your hands on your heart and say out loud, "I send love to this memory." Go through each memory, sending love to your memories in this way. Allow for emotional release and clearing so you can open yourself to feelings of resolution and peace.

- Choose one person you have hurt or betrayed, and make

amends to them. Conversely, choose someone who has been the source of your hurt and betrayal, and initiate the steps necessary to begin healing yourself from their offense(s). This may be accomplished through direct communication with the individual when possible, or as a therapeutic and interpersonal process of writing a letter to the person. Do not send the letter, but burn it in symbolic release as an offering to the universe/God/nature. Do this ritual as many times as is necessary to feel at peace. If you are still connected to this person, you may feel moved to share your letter with them. If you feel any kind of capitulation from them, you may be able to heal together.

If you have an unhealthy habit or addiction, outline steps to address it, and begin to enact those steps with the assistance of others. Awareness is the first step, and from this place of honesty one can outline a course of action with a support system of both natural supports (family and friends) and professional support (therapists, healers, twelve-step groups, peer-led groups, and treatment facilities). It's okay to ask for help. We all need help from others; there is *no* shame in reaching out to save your own life.

ᕽ *Affirmations*

"I forgive myself."
"There is enough for everyone."
"I love myself as I am."
"I am enough."
"Love opens all doors."

18

Medicine for the Soul

Transformation can, among other things, be compared to a fire burning away what once was. These experiences of change are the ones that leave us with deeply etched memories. It's through traversing and coming out on the other side of hardship that we, and life itself, take on more value. In those intense moments we know we are alive. When we are stretched to our limits, the skin of our emotions metaphorically gives way, and we expand from within, reaching beyond and through what we have known.

In the still moments of our existence when all is calm, there is often a longing for the visceral, passionate experiences of life. This is where our intention deepens and takes on more urgency. What I am describing may be moments of sheer bliss and heightened ecstasy, or memory imprints when our life changed unexpectedly beyond our immediate control.

The effects of what happens to change the landscape of our life may take some time to settle out. In the meantime, we are left to find our way through new terrain without a map. We may be thrust into change, literally in an instant, and we are left to figure things out on our own without the comfort and safety of what was once familiar to us.

I've met many women in recent years who shared with me that, as teenagers, they either left home or were forced out of their childhood home. I am one of those women. As a result of enduring events that I wasn't prepared for, I struggled for many years to find inner stability and to know my own value and worth. Situation after situation mirrored an aspect of traumatic losses that I incurred in adolescence, which affected my self-esteem and confidence.

As I look back now to that time in my life, I am grateful. Being stretched beyond my edges at a young age inspired me to eventually embrace my capacity to love deeply and unconditionally. I became resilient, and though I did not know it at that time, I also received profound lessons in forgiveness that were yet to unfold.

I was forced to grow up quickly in my childhood without the necessary self-care tools and coping skills. As a thirteen-year-old I turned to alcohol and drugs to cope with feelings of abandonment, fear, and loneliness. I assumed some adult responsibilities for my two younger siblings as my parents were going through their divorce. As an adult looking back on all this, I now know that my parents themselves must have been in a terrible place. They simply didn't have the skills to prioritize us then as they uncoupled.

I have come to understand that my parents were themselves wounded individuals who did the best that they knew how to do at the time. My heart is full of love and empathy for them now. My siblings and I have each had to come to terms with being responsible for our own recovery, and in our own way.

For me to fully heal, I discovered that I needed to flip my old self-damaging script by becoming a healing channel as an intuitive psychotherapist, artist, inventor, podcaster, and author. I have needed to share my vulnerabilities in order to heal through them. To restore myself to wholeness and reclaim my power, I have needed to speak my truth aloud and be witnessed. I've seen this process ring true for many others whom I know personally and have worked with professionally, and as a result, I encourage you to work hard to find your own voice.

By sharing our story with those who care to listen and be with us as we mend, I believe that we grow stronger in our broken places. With truly empathetic listening and the willingness to temporarily suspend our judgments, I know that we can encourage those we cross paths with to achieve their greatest potential.

It took me a number of years to understand that I had to be *willing* to assume responsibility for healing myself from the core wounds that left me feeling unworthy, undeserving, and depressed. I reenacted my wounds for many years, attracting people who triggered them, therefore reinforcing and supporting my limiting beliefs that were emblazoned with the message, "See how unworthy and unlovable you are?" Because of my unhealed psychoastrology, which stemmed from my core wounds, I developed a false belief that I was unwanted, lacked value, and was therefore disposable.

I am certain that some of you reading these words can relate to creating your life by default patterning, due to unhealed core wounding, resulting in a negative sense of your value, worth, and innate lovability. We have been told in greeting cards, memes, and talk shows that "time heals all wounds." However, it is not time simply passing that, in and of itself, heals us. It is what we do with our time as it passes that can heal us. If we embrace the need for transformation and strive to attain it, I know we can reach a place of inner peace from the deepest of wounds. Leaning in to my inner wisdom to find the silver lining of my own core wounding was a blessing and a gift that has taught me extraordinary principles about unconditional love and forgiveness. My parents and I have made amends, having had a number of necessary conversations over the years, and today we enjoy our shared time with each other. I was able to progressively forgive them once I could see Chiron's core wounding in them. As I've said, they too were suffering, and in need of their own self-forgiveness, empathy, and love. I'm blessed to be able to write this knowing that they will read it and understand my need to share it with you.

I'd like you to take a moment right now to get in touch with your own story of disempowerment resulting from your core wounding. Was it a particularly powerful life-changing moment you remember that may still cause you blame or shame? Settle in to that memory, and identify the experience that caused you to believe something untrue about yourself.

Please know that this false story you have told yourself about yourself can be transformed. You can grow through your past and become your best self, *if* you allow those sharp edges of experience to carve you into a person of love, compassion, forgiveness, and joy. What life skills have you gleaned from your core wounding? I've become adaptive, I have developed inner strength, and I am resourceful and authentic. These qualities afford me the clarity to skillfully counsel others to identify and embrace solution-focused outcomes during times of crisis and uncertainty.

We can learn to connect to our inner compass and confidence once we decide to heal our psychoastrology. You can do anything you put your full energy and resources toward. Do not waver from becoming the person you want to be. You can transform your core wounds and find happiness; you can recreate your life. We hold that power, and we must cherish and develop that inner capacity.

As human beings we tend to favor the status quo, not varying too far out of our predictable range and routine of experiences (our habitual orbiting patterns), lest we experience discomfort, anxiety, fear, uncertainty, or even panic. It is at this decision-making crossroads that we are free to choose what to do. Do we uncomfortably expand, being willing to go through the natural anxiety and fear, or do we contract into what is known? It is your choice to say yes or no to yourself, to your healing, to your happiness, and to the manifestation of your goals and your dreams.

I came to a crossroad and decided that I wanted the love within me to be greater than the hurt within me. I decided to permit myself to step fully into my power and inner beauty. You too must give yourself permission to enable what you really want.

Chiron's lessons have led me to the psychoastrology of my own core wounding, and because of that I am able to extend empathy to those of you who have felt unimportant, forgotten, rejected, unworthy, lost, and unlovable. I think that most of us have felt this range of emotion at one time or another in our lives. We wear masks and personas to conceal our pain and our disappointment in order to fit in. Writing this book over the last three and a half years has been a difficult journey emotionally because I am an empath and experientially have felt each placement of Chiron in my body as I researched and wrote about the twelve core woundings. I began to wonder if my desire to articulate and translate the themes of psychoastrology and core wounding were going to leave me feeling disconnected indefinitely.

I realized that the experience of feeling disconnected is one of the permeating effects of our core wounding, as is separation, isolation, and self-doubt. Let's face it—these core wounds are hard for us to even think about. However, left buried, our unhealed wounds obscure our clarity, separate us from our joy, and prevent us from being fully present in our lives. It's as if we lost a portion of our soul when we were wounded, and then we retrieve those parts through a healing process that is inspired by the act of empathetically forgiving ourselves.

My hope is that by sharing some of my story, you will likewise have the courage to transparently share yours, and this healing circle of being *witnessed* and *witnessing* will facilitate a change of consciousness one conversation at a time. Let's give ourselves permission to heal. Allow yourself to experience satisfaction and contentment through a consistent flow of receiving. Close the door to feeling unworthy, undeserving, and not good enough. Choose instead to internalize that "I am valuable, I am worthy, and I am loved unconditionally." You *are* in the perfect body to carry your soul and Spirit, you *have* the perfect mind to speak your thoughts, and you are *living* in the best place to have an influence. You are *right* where you need to be.

Sometimes when we begin to heal the psychoastrology of our core wounds and ask for an improvement in a current situation, the method of delivery may be disruptive and sent through unexpected experiences.

We may find ourselves escorted to both the edges of our emotional fortitude and the limits of our current coping skills.

This is because the minor planet of Chiron is mediated by Saturn—the planet of restriction, boundaries, and hard work—and by Uranus, the planet of unexpected and unforeseen changes. Saturn and Uranus apply the pressure needed to afford us the opportunity to choose whether we will allow Chiron's core wounds to transform us into a more conscious and evolved version of ourselves. Or do we choose to continue wounding others and hurting ourselves by being unconscious? There is a breakthrough nearby when we feel this tension, so hang on and be aware.

Some of us may turn to spirituality or angelic guides to help us find our way, our meaning, and our purpose. Others subscribe to randomness and chaos, and a shit-just-happens mentality. Still others believe in retribution from a god who is angry and judgmental, ready to punish at the slightest infraction.

I wrote this journal entry as a prayer and declaration to the universe on behalf of those who are still suffering, that they may find peace:

> *It does get better when the sun rises in your own heart.*
> *The grass will appear green again.*
> *Flowers will bloom in color, and you'll feel the blue sky on your skin.*
> *You will notice the wind at your back, not blowing sharply in your face anymore.*
> *The gray tone that once washed over your life gives way to color, sound, taste, smell, and texture.*
> *The ashes you rise from become fertile soil in which you lovingly plant the truth of who you now are. You become the most beautiful garden, blooming authentically.*
> *This is yours to create.*
> *May it be so, Amen.*

Our personal fulfillment is found by living both on the horizontal axis of physical existence in connection to others on Earth and through the vertical axis of spiritual existence in connection to that which is greater (the immaterial). It is true power to stand in a place of compassionate self-acceptance while leaning in to life's sharp edges with curiosity. I encourage you to be the loving presence you want to experience. We are in this together, and I am with you.

In conclusion, I leave you with two edifying quotes from *A Course in Miracles*. "Miracles occur naturally as expressions of love. The real miracle is the love that inspires them. In this sense everything that comes from love is a miracle." May the love in your heart create miracles in your life, and remember, "Miracles honor you because you are lovable. They dispel illusions about yourself and perceive the light in you. They thus atone (undo) for your errors by freeing you from your nightmares. By releasing your mind from the imprisonment of your illusions, they (miracles) restore your sanity."

Chiron and the Psychoastrology® of the United States of America

I am writing to the future of the United States of America and to our world that lies beyond this moment. Prompted by an experience riding home on the Los Angeles Metro tonight, I was moved to include this last and unplanned chapter. Life often inspires us to unexpected action if we are mindfully available to the present moment, free of judgment, and observing what is.

As I boarded the LA Metro subway system tonight, the only available seat faced backward, looking in the direction of where I was departing from (the past). I was zooming into the future at a fast speed, unable to slow it down or visually see my destination.

I immediately tuned in to the moment as a metaphor for certain junctures in life. I'm sure that if you're anything like me, at times you have lost your sense of direction. You may have felt lost, wondering where the train of your life was taking you. You may want to press the pause button so that you can catch your breath, gain your bearings, and take a time-out from it all. But we know that life moves as a powerful river, and we are the proverbial leaf being carried along by it.

In recent years I have learned that we can align our inner core self with the downstream momentum and flow of life, or we can try to go back to things as they were, furiously paddling upstream with resistance to what is, exhausting ourselves in the process. In this we also render ourselves unable to have present-moment awareness of the new landscape surrounding us, or the new destination that our river of life is flowing toward.

The United States of America is in one such powerful time of transition now, and this unprecedented time has required every one of us to change and adapt. The coronavirus disease 2019 (COVID-19) pandemic, which first came to light as a potential major disruptive force in China in December of 2019, has disrupted our nation and halted life as we knew it to be. The entire world has been brought together in a collective pause. People around the world are taking part in stay-at-home quarantine orders and precautions such as social distancing and wearing face masks in public.

Chiron as an astrological placement appears not only in the astrological birth chart of individual human beings, but also in the astrological birth chart of businesses, organizations, and countries. I thought it important to review the placement of Chiron in the birth chart of the United States to shed light on the psychoastrology that affects us as a country as we move into a post–COVID-19 world and into the election season of 2020. As I look into the psychoastrology of the United States of America, we will be under a Chiron in Aries influence again, just as we were when the Declaration of Independence was signed in 1776. Chiron was in the sign of Aries in the fourth house when our country approved the final text of the Declaration of Independence in Philadelphia, Pennsylvania, on July 4, 1776. Chiron in Aries reveals core wounding in our country's sense of value and worth. You would assume that the most powerful nation in the world would value its worth highly. So to understand the psychoastrology of Chiron of our nation, we must look at how this core wounding manifests in a fourth house placement.

The fourth house of America's psychoastrology pertains to our sense of home, security, nurturing, and family. This placement has to do with taking care of our own people. As generous as the United States of America has been and still is, we have sorely lacked in valuing the needs of our own inhabitants, especially during this global pandemic. According to the *Washington Post,* "by the time President Trump proclaimed himself a wartime president—and the Coronavirus the enemy—the United States was already on course to see more of its people die than in the wars of Korea, Vietnam, Afghanistan, and Iraq combined." Johns Hopkins University reports that due to COVID-19, in just four weeks (March 2020 to April 2020) "22 million Americans have filed for unemployment benefits. Technical glitches have prevented millions of Americans from receiving their stimulus checks from the U.S. Department of the Treasury, and the Small Business Administration, which supports U.S. Entrepreneurs with loans and funding, has run out of money for its Paycheck Protection Program." As I write this, the Centers for Disease Control and Prevention (CDC) reports the United States as the new epicenter of the COVID-19 outbreak.

Concordantly, in the presidential election of 2020, all of the issues illuminated by fourth house Chiron in Aries are at the forefront: economics, health care, education, children's rights, immigration, reproductive rights, climate change, crime prevention, and gun safety among them. How will a new parental figurehead lead the collective family of the United States?

Our next U.S. president will need to balance the scales of justice between how we as a nation mobilize resources to provide for the needs of others around the world and adequately nurture and protect our own American brothers and sisters here in the United States. We have the highest ranking in lethal crime among all industrialized nations, as documented in the book, *Crime Is Not the Problem.* According to the World Health Organization (WHO) data from 2010, the United States had the highest homicide rate of any country, over seven times higher than the average of other high-income countries, driven by a gun homicide rate that was 25.2 times higher. The United States Department of Veterans Affairs (VA) reported in 2016 that each day an average of twenty U.S. veterans commit suicide. These are servicemen and women who have protected our freedom, and they are tragically underserved.

Our next president will need to address the failing public school system, which is suffering in rural and urban areas. Some schools do not have functioning toilets, school supplies, or even books. The term *prison pipeline* has come of age in the lexicon of these communities where the educational needs of children are not being met. Research shows that a child who cannot read by the age of eight is less likely to graduate from high school and therefore has an increased chance of being incarcerated.

Our nation's food supply has been corrupted by the overuse of pesticides, herbicides, and fertilizers that leach nutrients from food and inject poisons into it. The overconsumption of sugar, which is a common food additive, is causing an epidemic of childhood obesity. These children end up being prescribed pharmaceuticals that promote dependence on medication before their developing brains are fully formed.

Homelessness is a major problem in our country. We have homeless children growing up in tent cities without adequate access to food, health care, or education. Many of our homeless have untreated mental illness and comorbid addiction issues.

The United States of America has aided countless millions of people around the world, including entire governments. However, concurrent with our country's core wounding by Chiron in the fourth house, we have a crisis in protecting and providing for the needs of our own people and the environment. For a country as powerful as the United States, these outcomes are exponential.

Chiron in Aries ushers in change—dramatic, visceral change—not for the faint of heart. My intention is that the next elected president of the United States in 2020 supports and protects the "unalienable rights" that the Declaration of Independence states has been given to *all humans* by their creator, and which governments are created to protect. I pray that this next president values these rights of all people in our beautiful melting pot of diversity to pursue "life, liberty and the pursuit of happiness."

Bibliography

Campbell, Joseph, with Bill Moyers. *The Power of Myth*. New York: Anchor Books, 1991.

Cartwright, Alexis. *Beyond Doorways: The Mysteries Revealed*. Australia: Transference Healing, 2008.

Casement, Patrick J. *Learning from the Patient*. New York: Guilford Press, 1991.

Chödrön, Pema. *When Things Fall Apart: Heart Advice for Difficult Times*. Boulder, Colo.: Shambhala Publishing, 2016.

Chopra, Deepak, and Rudolph E. Tanzi. *Super Brain: Unleashing the Explosive Power of Your Mind to Maximize Health, Happiness, and Spiritual Well-Being*. New York: Harmony Publishing, 2012.

Coleman, David. *The 26 Keys: The Magic of the Astral Light*. CreateSpace Independent Publishing Platform, 2011.

Crandell, Todd, and John Hanc. *Racing for Recovery: From Addict to Ironman*. Halcottsville, N.Y.: Breakaway Books. 2006.

Dalai Lama. *Ethics For the New Millennium*. New York: Riverhead Books. 1999.

Decker, Benjamin. *Practical Meditation for Beginners: 10 Days to a Happier, Calmer You*. Berkeley, Calif.: Althea Press, 2018.

Erikson, Erik H. *Childhood and Society*. New York: Norton, 1950.

Frey, William H., with Muriel Langseth. *Crying: The Mystery of Tears*. Winston-Salem, N.C.: Winston Pr., 1985.

Grant, Jan, and Jim Crawley. *Transference and Projection: Mirrors to the Self*. Buckingham, UK: Open University Press, 2002.

Hand Clow, Barbara. *Chiron: Rainbow Bridge between the Inner and Outer Planets*. St. Paul, Minn.: Llewellyn Publications, 1994.

Hay, Louise. *The Power Is Within You*. Carlsbad, Calif.: Hay House, 1991.

Herman, Judith L. *Trauma and Recovery*. New York: Basic Books, 1997.

Jung, C. G. *Memories, Dreams, Reflections*. New York: Pantheon Books, 1963.

Kessler, David. *Finding Meaning: The Sixth Stage of Grief*. New York: Scribner, 2019.

Kübler-Ross, Elisabeth. *On Death and Dying: What the Dying Have to Teach Doctors, Nurses, Clergy and Their Own Families*. New York: Scribner, 2014.

Kübler-Ross, Elisabeth, and David Kessler. *On Grief and Grieving: Finding the Meaning of Grief through the Five Stages of Loss*. New York: Simon and Schuster, 2005.

Lakhiani, Vishen. *The Code of the Extraordinary Mind*. Emmaus, Pa.: Rodale Books, 2016.

Leung, Mei-Keo, Way K. W. Lau, Chetwyn C. H. Chan, Samuel S. Y. Wong, Annis L. C. Fung, and Tatia M. C. Lee. "Meditation-induced neuroplastic changes in amygdala activity during negative affective processing." *Social Neuroscience* (April 10, 2017): 277–88.

Levine, Amir, and Rachel Heller. *Attached: The New Science of Adult Attachment and How It Can Help You Find–and Keep–Love*. New York: Penguin Group, 2010.

Masters, Robert Augustus. *Spiritual Bypassing: When Spirituality Disconnects Us from What Really Matters*. Berkeley, Calif.: North Atlantic Publishing, 2010.

Nadrich, Ora. *Says Who? How One Simple Question Can Change the Way You Think Forever*. New York: James Morgan Publishing, 2016.

Orloff, Judith. *The Empath's Survival Guide: Life Strategies for Sensitive People*. Boulder, Colo: Sounds True Publishing, 2017.

Prochaska, James O., and John C. Norcross. *Systems of Psychotherapy: A Transtheoretical Analysis*. Stamford, Conn.: Cengage Learning, 2013.

Rapp, C. *The Strengths Model: Case Management with People Suffering from Severe and Persistent Mental Illness*. 1st ed. New York: Oxford University Press, 1997.

Reinhart, Melanie. *Chiron and the Healing Journey*. London: Starwalker Press, 2010.

Schucman, Helen. *A Course in Miracles*. Mill Valley, Calif.: Foundation for Inner Peace, 1975.

Shakespeare, William. *Julius Caesar*. New York: Simon & Schuster, 2011.

Shinn, Florence Scovel. *The Wisdom of Florence Scovel Shinn*. New York: Simon and Schuster. 1989.

Thomas, Katherine Woodward. *Calling in the One: 7 Weeks to Attract the Love of Your Life*. New York: Harmony Publishing, 2004.

———. *Conscious Uncoupling: 5 Steps to Living Happily Even After*. New York: Harmony Books, 2015.

Williamson, Marianne. *A Year of Miracles: Tears to Triumph: The Spiritual Journey from Suffering to Enlightenment*. San Francisco: Harper One Publishing, 2017.

———. *A Year of Miracles: Daily Devotions and Reflections*. New York: Harper Collins, 2013.

Zimring, Franklin E., and Gordon Hawkins. *Crime Is Not the Problem: Lethal Violence in America*. Oxford: Oxford University Press, 1999.

Resources

Affirmations

Louise Hay: www.louisehay.com

Abraham-Hicks: www.abraham-hicks.com

Art

Matteo Neivert: www.matteoneivert.com

Astrologers and Astrology Websites

Carolyn Bufkin: www.carolynbufkin.com

Laurie St. Clare: www.sweetlifeastrology.com

Patricia Maher: www.patriciamaherastrology.wordpress.com

Rachel Lang: www.rachellangastrologer.com

American Federation of Astrologers: www.astrologers.com

AstroTheme: www.astrotheme.com

Cafe Astrology: www.cafeastrology.com

Empathic and Highly Sensitive People (HSP)

Dr. Judith Orloff: www.drjudithorloff.com

Energy Medicine

Brandy Gillmore, Ph.D.: www.brandygillmore.com

Dr. Sue Morter: www.drsuemorter.com

Grief and Loss

David Kessler: www.grief.com

Elisabeth Kübler-Ross: www.ekrfoundation.org

Meditation

Deepak Chopra: www.chopracentermeditation.com (particularly Oprah & Deepak 21-Day Meditation Experience)

Pema Chödrön: www.pemachodronfoundation.org

Ben Decker: www.bendeckermeditation.com

The Honest Guys Meditations: youtube.com/TheHonestGuys

Miscellaneous Astrology and Healing

Jeremy Neal: www.chirotic.com

David Osborn: www.greekmedicine.net

GreekMythology: www.greekmythology.com

Healing Universe Professional ethical Tarot and Astrology: www.healinguniverse.com

Planet Waves: www.planetwaves.net

Open Mind Training and Institute

Dr. Ronald Alexander: www.ronaldalexander.com

Physical Health

Ann Boroch: www.annboroch.com

Leilani Heno: www.x-trainers.com

Amy Simonetta: www.asiendurance.com

Psychotherapy/Counseling/ Life Coaching

Nikki Eisenhauer, LLC-Life Coach: www.nikkieisenhauer.com

Bridget Falcon, LPC: www.neworleanstherapist.com

Prem Glidden, Transformational Coach: www.premglidden.com

Marisa Peer: www.marisapeer.com

Dr. Melissa Richman: www.richmancare.com

Jamie Lerner, LCSW: www.jamie-lerner.com

Dani Rukin LPCC, CPCC: www.danirukin.com

Nina Watt, LPC, LMFT: www.ninawatt.com

Reiki/Psychic Healers/Mediums/ Angel Practitioners

Rachel Collier: www.waychilllife.com

Julianna Davis: www.healingwithjules.com

Candy Claire Hough: www.angelhealinghouse.com

Dr. Sarah Larsen: www.drsarahlarsen.com

Mark Mezadourian: www.markmezadourian.com

Tison Lui: www.tisonthehealer.com

Relationship Coaching and Therapy

Katherine Woodward Thomas: www.katherinewoodwardthomas.com; www
.callingintheonecourse.com; www.consciousuncoupling.com

John Gray, Ph.D.: www.marsvenus.com

Corey Folsom: www.CoreRelationship.com

Sound Healing

Lauren Waggoner: www.peacelovesoundology.com

Spiritual Transformation

Marianne Williamson: www.marianne.com

Thought Coaching

Ora Nadrich: www.oranadrich.com

Women's Empowerment

Catherine Gray: www.360karma.com

Tracy Lee Jones: www.tracyleejones.com

Ingrid Arna: www.ingridarna.com

Index

About the Author

Lisa Tahir is from New Orleans, Louisiana, where she became a Licensed Clinical Social Worker (LCSW) in 2000. She expanded her practice to Los Angeles, California, in 2014, and attained her second LCSW license in California in 2016. She is additionally certified in EMDR level I, in Reiki level II, and as a Thought Coach through the Institute for Transformational Thinking in Los Angeles, California. Lisa has private practice office locations and residences in both Los Angeles and New Orleans, and she lives between both cities with her cats Jiggy and Baby.

Lisa is passionately committed to working with people to help them heal through all of the senses of the body by utilizing intuition, therapy, energy healing, meditation, Reiki healing, crystal healing, nutrition, sound frequencies, yoga, exercise, podcasting, writing, and teaching. She enjoys speaking on topics related to psychoastrology, spirituality, emotional health, physical health, and mental well-being.

Lisa loves maintaining her fitness through many self-care practices and activities that range from meditation, reading, writing, and creating glass art to running, indoor rock climbing, yoga, surfing, traveling, weight lifting, and spending time with family, friends, and loved ones.

She hosts the popular weekly podcast *All Things Therapy* found on LA Talk Radio, iTunes, Google Play, iHeartRADIO, Stitcher, YouTube, and other places where podcasts are found.

Please reach out to schedule individual, couple, and group intuitive psychotherapy sessions; request media appearances, interviews, and speaking engagements; or learn more about your personal Chiron through her one-on-one intensive psychoastrology monthly coaching program. Below are the websites and social media sites where you can learn more about and connect with Lisa Tahir, including her nonprofit, The "Yes" Foundation, INC. It uses tax-deductible donations to teach children and adults with disabilities to blow and cast glass art utilizing her ADA compliant and US patented workbench, "The CHAIR-iot."

Website: www.nolatherapy.com
Podcast: *All Things Therapy,* www.latalkradio.com/content /all-things-therapy
Twitter: www.twitter.com/TahirLcsw
Facebook: www.facebook.com/nolatherapy; www.facebook .com/TheYESfoundation
LinkedIn: www.linkedin.com/in/lisatahir
Instagram: www.instagram.com/nolatherapy
YouTube: www.youtube.com/nolatherapy
Patreon: www.patreon.com/allthingstherapy

Books of Related Interest

Waking Up in 5D
A Practical Guide to Multidimensional Transformation
by Maureen J. St. Germain

Opening the Akashic Records
Meet Your Record Keepers and Discover Your Soul's Purpose
by Maureen J. St. Germain

Astrology Reading Cards
Your Personal Guidance from the Stars
by Alison Chester-Lambert, MA
Illustrated by Richard Crookes

Aspects in Astrology
A Guide to Understanding Planetary Relationships in the Horoscope
by Sue Tompkins

Astrology and the Rising of Kundalini
The Transformative Power of Saturn, Chiron, and Uranus
by Barbara Hand Clow

Reclaiming Life after Trauma
Healing PTSD with Cognitive-Behavioral Therapy and Yoga
by Daniel Mintie, LCSW and Julie K. Staples, Ph.D.

The Book of Ho'oponopono
The Hawaiian Practice of Forgiveness and Healing
by Luc Bodin, M.D., Nathalie Bodin Lamboy, and Jean Graciet

Scripting the Life You Want
Manifest Your Dreams with Just Pen and Paper
by Royce Christyn
Foreword by Mitch Horowitz

INNER TRADITIONS • BEAR & COMPANY
P.O. Box 388
Rochester, VT 05767
1-800-246-8648
www.InnerTraditions.com

Or contact your local bookseller